WE DEMAND
THE RIGHT TO VOTE
The Journey to the 19th Amendment

" *MAKE THE WORLD BETTER,* "
SAID SUFFRAGE PIONEER LUCY STONE.

Meredie Moll

Failure is Impossible

WE DEMAND
THE RIGHT TO VOTE
The Journey to the 19th Amendment

Written & Illustrated by Meneese Wall

Paxton Press
Santa Fe, New Mexico

There is no history about which there is so much ignorance
as this great movement for the establishment of equal political rights of women.[1]
Susan B. Anthony
1820 – 1906

ISBN: 978-1-7349010-0-9 (paperback)
Library of Congress Control Number: 2020908176

First published in 2020
Printed in the United States of America

Cover Artwork: *Columbia* by Meneese Wall
Book design by Meneese Wall & Katerine Contreras
Book Interior Artwork by Meneese Wall
Edited by Beth Crosby

Paxton Press
Post Office Box 9437
Santa Fe, NM 87504
www.paxtonpress.com

Notice: The information in this book is true and complete to the best of the author's knowledge. This book is offered without guarantee on the part of the author, who disclaims all liability in connection with the use of this book.

There will never be a new world order until women are a part of it.[2]

Alice Paul
1885 – 1977

Liberty

Contents

Don't dare to say you are free until all women are free.[3]

Inez Milholland
1886 – 1916

WE DEMAND THE RIGHT TO VOTE

The Journey to the 19th Amendment

Suffrage Superhero

Introduction

We Demand the Right to Vote: The Journey to the 19th Amendment introduces the reader to the American women's civil rights movement known as "Women's Suffrage." The following pages recount the work of some of America's most influential national leaders who motivated thousands of women—and men—at the local, state, regional, and national levels to work for women's rights. Passage of the Nineteenth Amendment involved the efforts of countless individuals and groups, both named and unknown, to obtain the legal right for all women to vote.

Starting with the influence of freedoms enjoyed by women in Native American cultures, *We Demand The Right To Vote* explores women's conventions, arrests, trials, petitions, battles won, and those lost to reveal society's slow acceptance of women's involvement outside of their socially prescribed realm. Women's fight to secure their power to vote took almost three generations and required courage, tenacity, sacrifice, agitation, and demands.

We Demand The Right To Vote is an overview of this pivotal time in American history, which has been left out of our history books, cultural stories, and classrooms. The author hopes this book inspires Americans of all ages to learn more about this important chapter in our collective history.

Every woman deserves the liberty to choose her own life's path, to find and claim her own power, and ultimately to be her own superhero. Demand it of yourself. Demand it of the world you live in.

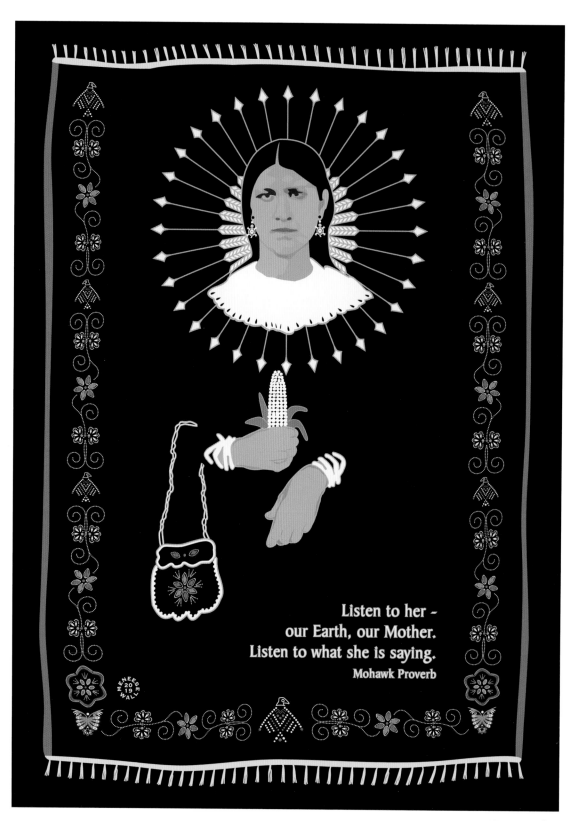

Native Wisdom

The Founding of Our Nation

1776

Imagine you're told how to dress and how to act, what you can and cannot say, where your speech is and is not appropriate, and whether you can or cannot legally own anything. That was the reality of our foremothers in 1776, with little recourse to change their situation. At the same time, our forefathers were similarly restricted by England without a say. These male forebears, however, decided they no longer desired "to eat the bread of dependence"[4] upon another power. They rebelled against their English persecutors, who sought to "deny them the right of representation in the government." In the "very first paragraph of … the Declaration [of Independence] is the assertion of the natural right of all to the ballot,"[5] arming them with a remedy to this egregious wrong. "For how can 'the consent of the governed' be given if the right to vote be denied?"[6]

Though these assertions could have been proclaimed by any one of our country's founders about their frustrations with English domination, they were in fact declared by suffrage pioneer Susan B. Anthony about women's lack of equal treatment under the laws of the United States, a century and more after our country's founders signed their rebellious Declaration of Independence.

In the eighteenth and nineteenth centuries, white men of the United States created the laws that regulated society. By common practice, their children identified themselves through their father's lineage, and women had few rights. When a woman married, her rights were taken away by law and given to her husband. Post nuptials, she couldn't own property, enter into contracts, sign legal documents, dictate how her wages were spent or have control over her children. She was also denied the opportunity to obtain an education equal to her male counterparts.

It was considered scandalous for a woman to give a speech in public, especially to both men and women. She was deemed the weaker sex and expected to be "ladylike" while accepting lower wages than a man for the same job. She was denied the right to vote, which would have given her the opportunity to make changes to the laws that subjugated her. At the founding of our country, only property-owning white males were privileged with the vote. New Jersey was the only exception. There, women and blacks could vote until 1807, when the state legislature changed the law to restrict suffrage to only free, tax-paying, white male citizens.

In contrast, America's Native Iroquois population in upper New York State lived under a very different social structure of self-government. The Iroquois Confederacy, also called Six Nations, consisted of the Mohawk, Onondaga, Oneida, Cayuga, Seneca, and

The world has never yet seen a truly great and virtuous nation because in the degradation of woman, the very fountains of life are poisoned at their source.[7]

Lucretia Mott
1793 – 1880

Tuscarora tribes. Their women owned the land, their homes, and the rights to their children. They could gamble, join medical societies, participate in political ceremonies, vote, and veto wars. Though Iroquois leaders (chiefs) were men, and their tribal councils dominated by men, the women nominated council members and held the power to remove them should the men not properly fulfill their responsibilities. Iroquois children traced their lineage through their mothers. Husbands joined their wives' clans, and all men were expected to treat women with respect. Violence against women and children was not tolerated.

The men hunted and prepared the fields for the Three Sisters—corn, beans, and squash—while the women tended the crops. Within their fenced villages, multiple groups of matrilineally related families shared wooden longhouses and slept in bunk beds, an invention of their people.

The Native and American cultures had long shared regular trade, cultural exchanges, and friendship. Undoubtedly, the Iroquois way of life showed American women they could do more and have a larger say in governing their own people.

The Dare for Change

Seneca Falls Convention

Seventy-two years after Americans declared independence from England, American women's status in society remained unchanged. They continued to be taxed without representation and denied access to the ballot. These were just two areas where women were politically repressed. In the social realm, common practices toward women needed change that legislation could not address such as dress reform, equal education, and norms of public conduct. Elizabeth Cady Stanton, Lucretia Mott, and others decided to take steps to better women's lives.

While attending the first World Anti-Slavery Convention in London on her honeymoon in 1840, Elizabeth Cady Stanton met Lucretia Mott, one of the first women she had ever known "who believed in the equality of the sexes."[8] Mott was a Quaker preacher and worked for many causes including Native American Rights, abolition, and women's rights. She and Stanton "resolved to hold a convention as soon as they returned...to advocate for the rights of women."[9]

The next eight years passed with the two women otherwise occupied. Mott traveled widely in support of her causes. Stanton committed herself to studying "law, history, and political economy."[10] Her father was a lawyer, politician, and judge, so she learned firsthand how few rights women possessed under the law. During that eight-year span, she gave birth to the first three of her seven children and recognized "the wearied, anxious look of the majority of women...[It] impressed me with a strong feeling that some active measures should be taken to remedy the wrongs of society in general, and of women in particular."[11] She read books on women's rights by noted writers and philosophers including Mary Wollstonecraft's *A Vindication of the Rights of Women*, Sarah Moore Grimké's *Letters on the Equality of the Sexes and the Condition of Woman,* and Margaret Fuller's *Woman in the Nineteenth Century.*"[12]

In 1848, Stanton and Mott had tea with Mary McClintock, Martha Coffin Wright (Lucretia Mott's sister), and Jane C. Hunt in Waterloo, New York, and together decided "to do and dare anything"[13] toward the advancement of women's rights. They worked on a "Declaration of Sentiments," with Stanton as the primary author. The work was modeled after the Declaration of Independence and asserted "that all men *and women* are created equal," reiterating that both genders "are endowed by their Creator with certain inalienable rights."[14] They argued that women were oppressed by the government and the patriarchal society in which they lived and listed sixteen facts as evidence of that oppression including women's lack of representation in the government, their lack of property rights in marriage, and their inequality in divorce law, education, and employment opportunities. The most controversial item was the call for women's suffrage—the right

The history of the past is but one long struggle upward to equality.[15]

Elizabeth Cady Stanton
1815 – 1902

to vote—"[T]he right by which all other [rights] can be secured," Stanton wrote. [16]

They posted a newspaper notice in the *Seneca County Courier* for a "convention to discuss the social, civil, and religious condition and rights of women" [17] on July 19th and 20th. Three hundred people attended the Wesleyan Chapel meeting in Seneca Falls, New York, to hear what the women had to say. Forty-seven men, including Frederick Douglass—a former slave turned eloquent speaker for the abolition of slavery, racial equality, and women's rights, also attended the convention. It's important to note that no black women attended. They campaigned for women's suffrage in churches rather than conventions until later in the movement because of social segregation of the time.

Stanton read aloud their work, the "Declaration of Sentiments and Resolutions," which "demand[ed] the equal station [for women] to which they are entitled." It further stated, "the history of mankind is a history of repeated injuries and usurpations on the part of man toward woman, having in direct object the establishment of an absolute tyranny over her." [18]

Sixty-eight women and thirty-two men signed their acceptance of the declaration, thereby challenging the legal and social structures of the day. They acknowledged "in entering upon the great work before us, we anticipate no small amount of misconception, misrepresentation, and ridicule; but we shall use every instrumentality within our power to effect our object." [19]

Soon thereafter, C. Tompkins, with music arranger Julia F. Baker, wrote lyrics about these important times in the "Women's Rights Convention Waltz," and Kate Horn composed "Women's Rights: A Ballad" in 1853. Many newspaper accounts supported the movement, but not all. *The Rochester Adviser* said, "To us they appear extremely dull and uninteresting, and, aside from their novelty, hardly worth notice." [20] The *Lowell (Massachusetts) Courier* claimed that women wanted to be men, but "they should have resolved at the same time, that it was obligatory also upon [the men] to wash dishes, ... handle the broom, darn stockings, ... look beautiful, and be as fascinating as those blessed morsels of humanity God gave to preserve that rough animal man .... " Stanton continued to call for women's right to vote declaring, "The right is ours. Have it we must. Use it we will." [21]

History might forever debate what constituted the start of the American Women's Civil Rights Movement, but like so much in life, the movement was a process not an event. The Seneca Falls Convention can certainly lay claim to being the first major public convention devoted entirely to women's rights, although many women's anti-slavery conventions predated Seneca Falls. No doubt these gatherings helped build women's confidence in their own voice and social contributions, thereby building momentum to this key 1848 meeting.

Lucretia Mott

Lucretia Mott

1793 – 1880

"Woman has never wakened to her highest destinies and holiest hopes," said Lucretia Mott. "The time is coming when educated females will not be satisfied with the present objects of their low ambition...sinking down into almost useless inactivity...the social circle...a little sewing, a little reading, a little domestic duty...." As she proclaimed in her speech, "Discourse On Woman," Mott knew women would have to facilitate critical social change. "There is nothing of greater importance to the well-being of society at large...than the true and proper position of woman." [22] She boldly announced during the talk in December 1849, "A new generation of women is now upon the stage."

Lucretia Mott was a powerful orator, which was somewhat surprising given her petite build and conservative Quaker attire. She was also a pacifist and staunch abolitionist. During a speech addressing a group of white male medical students in Philadelphia, she challenged the young men to question the prevailing religious and societal wisdom of the day by unabashedly stating, "I am a worshiper after the way called heresy, a believer after the manner which many deem infidel." [23] Mott was referring to her stance against slavery, in spite of the fact that enslaving blacks was a common practice. She used "the striking contrast between her virtuous femininity and her anti-slavery radicalism" [24] to influence these future leaders, and many others like them, to facilitate social change away from slavery. Quakers "believed...God's spirit dwelled within each person, regardless of sex, race, or class," [25] so she considered slavery evil. Mott knew women couldn't abolish slavery on their own. They needed to convince men of abolition's wisdom as well. To do that, women needed to change men's minds about women's place in society. This conversion was difficult because "culture dictated that women [were to] serve as the moral counterpart for the male world of business and politics." [26]

As "one of the most famous women in America," [27] Lucretia Mott spoke out for women's right to choose their path in a time when few agreed with this notion or questioned women's place in society. Many women disagreed with the movement to change the role of women in society.

"[Woman will] not be limited by man...," Mott said, "nor will [she] fulfill less her domestic relations... [Woman] will not suffer herself to be degraded into a mere dependent." [28] Preaching against slavery and advocating for women's rights was radical for the times, especially coming from a woman. But these were Mott's passions, and with her husband's support, they were her missions in life.

The former Lucretia Coffin was born on the island of Nantucket off the coast of Massachusetts, one of three children born to Anna Folger Coffin and Thomas Coffin.

It is not the intelligent woman v. the ignorant woman; nor the white woman v. the black, the brown, and the red, it is not even the cause of woman v. man. Nay, tis woman's strongest vindication for speaking that the world needs to hear her voice.[29]

Anna Julia Cooper
1858 – 1964

After her family moved to Boston in 1804, the then thirteen-year-old Lucretia transferred to Nine Partners School, a Quaker school in Dutchess County, New York. "It exposed her to the tensions between Quaker simplicity and prosperity, their anti-slavery testimony and the slave economy, and their connections to the larger society."[30] Upon graduation, she remained at Nine Partners to become a teacher. She learned firsthand about the pay inequality between male and female instructors. Women were paid significantly less. This lit a fire in her to campaign for women's rights alongside abolition. In 1809, Lucretia moved with her family to Philadelphia. James Mott, another Nine Partners teacher, soon followed, and in 1811, he and Lucretia married and reared their six children there.

Lucretia Mott was unafraid to take a bold stance for her causes. To protest slavery, she participated in the Free Produce Movement, refusing to wear or eat the products of slavery. Along with black women in 1833, she helped found the Philadelphia Female Anti-Slavery Society opposed to slavery and racism and faced mob violence, though not injured, for her stance. Mott believed the Bible supported women's rights and valiantly proclaimed that God "gave dominion to both [man and woman] over the lower animals, but not to one [man] over the other [woman]."[31] She was part of the Free Religious Association with Ralph Waldo Emerson and others to "emancipate religion from the dogmatic traditions it had been previously bound to."[32]

Mott spoke at the Seneca Falls Convention, traveled widely giving speeches for women's rights and served as president of the American Equal Rights Association, which advocated for universal suffrage. In 1864 she helped found Swarthmore College, named for the city where it stands in Pennsylvania.

THE LILY

FIRST NEWSPAPER DEVOTED TO THE INTERESTS OF WOMEN
FIRST NEWSPAPER OWNED, EDITED & PUBLISHED BY A WOMAN

THE COSTUME OF WOMEN
SHOULD BE SUITED
TO HER WANTS AND NECESSITIES
...
LET MEN BE COMPELLED
TO WEAR OUR DRESS FOR AWHILE
AND WE SHOULD SOON HEAR THEM
ADVOCATING A CHANGE

AMELIA BLOOMER

Amelia Bloomer

Dress Reform

1849

"Any great change must expect opposition, because it shakes the very foundation of privilege,"[33] Lucretia Mott said. She wasn't alone in this realization or its multilayered consequences for women's lives. Elizabeth Smith Miller—daughter of antislavery philanthropist Gerrit Smith and abolitionist Ann Carroll Fitzhugh Smith, second cousin of Elizabeth Cady Stanton, and Upstate New York resident—understood the critical need to liberate society's disenfranchised. She also championed women's rights. Toward that end, Miller advocated for dress reform—away from women's Victorian fashion with its functional restraints—toward clothing designed for comfort and ease of movement. Miller proclaimed, "[T]his shackle should no longer be endured,"[34] referring not only to women's clothing per se but also to its iconography of women's overall dominance by their chauvinistic society.

The loose-fitting tunics and leggings worn by the Oneida Nation's women inspired Miller, and she decided to substitute part of her own "heavy, untidy, and exasperating old garment [with a pair of] Turkish trousers to the ankle with a skirt reaching some four inches below the knee."[35] This new fashion ensemble "was first introduced at the various 'water cures,'"[36] spa towns that promoted cures for a range of health problems through water therapies. Proprietors of the "water cures" welcomed "sick and delicate women, often rendered so by their unhealthful mode of dress," to wear the new relaxed garb since the owners were "in touch with all reform movements, and their hospitality was freely extended to those engaged in them."[37] Countless women worldwide embraced this radical costume liberation called "bloomers," named for Amelia Bloomer who popularized them in 1849 in her newspaper, *The Lily*, the first paper devoted to the interests of women and the first nineteenth-century paper owned, edited, and published by a woman.

While men's attire was relatively loose-fitting, a woman's outer dress covered several layers of undergarments, topped by a corset hooked in the front, laced in the back, and stiffened with "boning" made of strips of whalebone or metal. The outer dress was cinched in to produce an hourglass figure with a tiny waist, accentuated by wide skirts rendered so by "heavy, quilted and stiffly-starched petticoats, five or six worn at a time."[38] A woman's underclothes alone could weigh as much as 14 pounds. Not only were the physical restrictions of corsets uncomfortable, they were potentially dangerous to a woman's health, causing poor blood circulation, fainting, curvature of the spine, and deformities of the ribs.

In the spring of 1851, Amelia Bloomer introduced Elizabeth Cady Stanton to Susan B.

It will not do to say that it is out of woman's sphere to assist in making laws, for if that were so then it should be also out of her sphere to submit to them.[39]

Amelia Jenks Bloomer
1818 – 1894

Anthony when all were attending an anti-slavery meeting. Of that meeting, Stanton wrote, "There [Anthony] stood, with her good, earnest face and genial smile...I liked her thoroughly." [40] Stanton and Anthony soon embraced the new "rational dress" [41] with enthusiasm. The two lived the rest of their lives as friends and pioneers for the women's suffrage movement, giving countless speeches in communities across the nation and inspiring thousands of other women, and men, to join in the fight for women's rights.

Songs and dances celebrated women's newfangled sartorial freedom with such tunes as "The New Bloomer Schottische," "The Bloomer Waltz," and "The Bloomer Polka"—not to be confused with "Real Bloomer Polka." The "Bloomer Promenading Waltz" and "The Bloomer's Complaint" also celebrated the fashion. Most of society, however, was not ready for such a radical shift, and music supported that point of view as well with the "Anti-Bloomer Schottische."

Men especially found the fashion change an affront to their authority. Though the two suffrage pioneers wore bloomers for a few years, they finally had to leave dress reform to future generations because the attire distracted audiences from their message: Women were citizens and as such deserved the right to vote.

Bloomers would make a fashion comeback within the next few decades.

Amelia Jenks Bloomer (1818–1894) was born in Homer, New York, to Ananias Jenks and Lucy Webb Jenks, a family of modest means. Bloomer received little formal education. At twenty-two, she married Dexter Bloomer—a writer, newspaper publisher, and politician—who encouraged his wife to write for his newspaper, the *Seneca County Courier*. From 1849 to 1853, Amelia published *The Lily*, which first covered the temperance movement and later expanded to articles about women's rights. In 1853, she sold the paper and moved to Iowa with her husband. Amelia Bloomer lectured for many years in favor of temperance and women's rights.

Sojourner Truth

Sojourner Truth

Restrictive clothing affected women of all ethnicities, but women of African descent had more pressing issues for improving their lives, chief among them slavery, lack of education, and racial subjugation. Sojourner Truth was one such woman, and she played an important role in the history of the abolitionist and women's civil rights movements.

Often what we know as history is not historically accurate. Such is the case with the quote in this chapter's artwork, "Ain't I a woman?"[42] attributed to Sojourner Truth from an extemporaneous speech she gave on racial inequalities to a women's rights convention in Akron, Ohio, in 1851. Since Truth was illiterate, her speech was not written down; however, her good friend and journalist Marius Robinson[43] took notes, which were published a week later in the *Anti-Slavery Bugle*. The article made no mention of this line. Twelve years later, during the Civil War, the *New York Independent* published another version of her speech in 1863, this time giving Sojourner a Southern accent, with this statement as the speech's central theme. Truth was a six-foot-tall New Yorker, whose first language was Dutch. She started learning English at age nine, so it's unlikely she spoke like a Southern slave. "It is interesting to note that Marius Robinson and Sojourner Truth were good friends and it was documented that they went over his [Frances Gage's] transcription of her speech before he published it. One could infer from this pre printing meeting, that even if he did not capture every word she said, that she must have blessed his transcription and given permission to print her speech in the *Anti-Slavery Bugle*."[44]

Truth's speech encouraged men to give women their civil rights. "I have heard much about the sexes being equal. I can carry as much as any man, and I can eat as much too, if I can get it ... The poor men seem to be all in confusion. They don't know what to do. Why, children [referring to men], if you have woman's rights, give it to her, and you will feel better. You have your own rights, and they won't be so much trouble ... Women are coming up; blessed be God ... ."[45]

Sojourner Truth (1797 – 1883) was born a slave named Isabelle "Belle" Baumfree, in Ulster County, New York, about 1797; the exact year is unknown. By age 13, she'd been bought and sold three times. Of her five children, four by her enslaved husband Thomas and one by a slave owner, only her infant Sophia, her husband's child, remained with her when she escaped to freedom in 1826. Quakers helped her find a home with an abolitionist family, the Van Wageners, in New Paltz, New York.

That same year, Belle learned that her son Peter had been sold out of state, which was against New York law. The Van Wageners helped her sue in court to get her son back. She

We are all bound up together in one great bundle of humanity, and society cannot trample on the weakest and feeblest of its members without receiving the curse in its own soul.[46]

Frances Harper
1825 – 1911

was one of the first black women to successfully sue a white man.

In 1843, Belle became a Methodist and asked the Lord to give her a new name symbolic of her new mission—to travel about and proclaim the truth, ergo, Sojourner Truth. The next year she joined the Northampton Association of Education and Industry in Northampton, Massachusetts. Members of the organization lived on 470 acres and supported women's rights, religious tolerance, and pacifism. While there, Truth met other well-known abolitionists who also supported women's rights including Frederick Douglass and William Lloyd Garrison. In 1850, Truth started dictating her memoir to her friend Olive Gilbert. Garrison published Truth's book, *The Narrative of Sojourner Truth* the same year.

Truth spent the rest of her life as an abolitionist and suffrage activist, meeting and speaking with some of the most influential leaders in those movements. To one raucous crowd, she said, "You may hiss as you please, but women will get their rights anyway. You can't stop us, neither." [47] Some of her views were considered radical even within the abolitionist community. Truth advocated for political equality for all women—black and white, civil rights for black women as well as men, and warned that women's rights would fade from the political realm after black men could legally vote. "I tell you I can't read a book, but I can read de people." [48] During the Civil War, Truth helped to recruit black men to fight for the Union Army. She even met with Presidents Abraham Lincoln and Ulysses S. Grant at the White House. Truth died in 1883 at her home in Michigan at age 86.

HARRIET TUBMAN

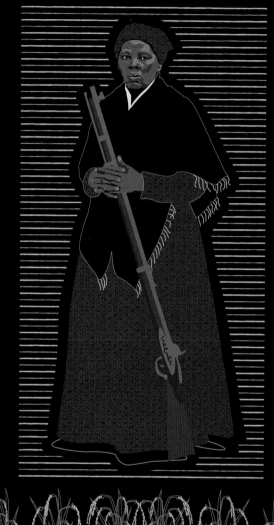

UNDERGROUND RAILROAD CONDUCTOR

EVERY GREAT DREAM BEGINS WITH A DREAMER

Harriet Tubman

Harriet Tubman

1860

Supporters of women's equal rights often started as abolitionists, including Mott, Stanton, Anthony, and Lucy Stone. The issue of slavery was a divisive political issue from the beginning of our country, and by the 1860s most northern states were against it, while Southern states were dependent on it for the financial viability of their large plantations. President Abraham Lincoln said, "Slavery is founded in the selfishness of man's nature—opposition to it is his love of justice."[49]

Many slaves escaped to freedom by way of the Underground Railroad, a network of secret routes and safe houses that guided slaves to freedom in the North. "I was the conductor of the Underground Railroad for eight years," said Tubman, "and I can say what most conductors can't say—I never ran my train off the track and I never lost a passenger."

Of course, no one chose to be a slave, and in the seventeenth, eighteenth, and nineteenth centuries, slave owners often employed extreme measures to deter slave defection. Whipping, branding, maiming, forced wearing of heavy iron collars—some with bells, and manacles were just a few of the techniques used. Laws prohibiting education, travel, and even swimming also kept slaves dependent on their servile position for survival.

Harriet Tubman (1821–1913) was named Araminta "Minty" Ross when she was born into slavery in eastern Maryland about 1821. Hers was a life of countless hardships and cruelty. When Minty was five or six years old, her owners hired her out to watch over a white woman's baby as it slept. Whenever the baby cried, her owners severely whipped Minty. When she was a teen, an overseer threw a 2-pound weight at another slave standing nearby and hit Minty in the head. The blow cracked her skull, injuring her brain and causing lifelong narcolepsy and temporal lobe epilepsy.

In 1844, Minty Ross married John Tubman, a black man who was born free and worked temporary jobs. They met on the plantation where Minty was enslaved. Within their first year of marriage, the plantation's owner died, leaving his heirs to pay off huge debts. Minty feared she might be sold to help settle those debts, so she ran away. Her husband did not join her. The neighboring county had a sizable Quaker community who provided refuge to runaway slaves and helped them navigate the Underground Railroad to freedom in Philadelphia. "Quakers almost as good as colored," Tubman said. "They call themselves friends, and you can trust them every time."[50] Once free, Minty chose a new name to symbolize her fresh start—Harriet, her mother's name, along with her husband's surname. Harriet Tubman's work with the Underground Railroad introduced her to many of the nineteenth century's prominent reformers for abolition and women's

Virtue knows no color line.[51]

Ida B. Wells
1862 – 1931

rights. Relationships with Lucretia Mott, Susan B. Anthony, Martha Coffin Wright, Frances Harper, Frederick Douglass, and others helped Tubman grow her ideologies while also receiving personal and financial support for her anti-slavery missions.

In 1850, and for the next ten years, Tubman returned to Maryland to bring at least seventy slaves, including family members, to freedom, earning her the nickname "Moses." In 1859, she moved to Auburn, New York, and became a community activist, humanitarian, and suffragist. Tubman attended numerous local and national suffrage conventions. In 1896, she spoke and sang at the first convention of the National Association of Colored Women. The next year, she was a delegate to the Twenty-Ninth Annual New York State Women's Suffrage Association convention in Geneva, New York.

Tubman worked for the Union Army during the Civil War as a scout, spy, and nurse, where she helped free hundreds more slaves. Though illiterate, Tubman never shied away from making speeches for women's suffrage rights and abolition. In her final years, Harriet Tubman lived on a 25-acre parcel abutting her home in Auburn, New York, that she purchased at auction. It was named the Tubman Home for Aged and Indigent Negroes. Prior to her death in 1913, she deeded the property to the African Methodist Episcopal Zion Church for them to carry on her humanitarian work.

Do All You Can, No Matter What, to Get People to Think.

Elizabeth Cady Stanton

Elizabeth Cady Stanton

1815 – 1902

"Tag you're it" proclaimed the newly married 24-year-old Elizabeth Cady Stanton to her sister's husband Daniel on the decks of the ship *Montreal*. "[Daniel] and I had had for years a standing game of 'tag' at all our partings," wrote Elizabeth, "and he had vowed to send me 'tagged' to [my honeymoon in] Europe. I was equally determined that he should not. Accordingly, I had a desperate chase after him all over the vessel, but...[h]e had the last 'tag' and escaped...[having] the advantage of height, long limbs, and freedom from skirts, I really stood no chance whatever. However, as the chase kept us all laughing, it helped to soften the bitterness of parting." [52]

The sparkling Elizabeth Cady Stanton was born in Johnstown, located in New York's lush Mohawk Valley, forty miles northwest of Albany. Plump and curious with curly dark hair and blue eyes, Elizabeth was the eighth child of Margaret Livingston Cady's and Daniel Cady's eleven children. Her father was a prominent, wealthy attorney who served one term in the United States Congress. Five of Elizabeth's siblings died in childhood or infancy, leaving her parents with five daughters and one son, Eleazar. As was the law and custom of the time, the son was to inherit all. But when Eleazar died at age twenty, Daniel Cady was devastated. Elizabeth, eleven at the time, was determined to show her father that she could be just as accomplished as a boy and set out "to be learned and courageous." [53]

She graduated as the only girl from Johnstown Academy and went on to Troy Female Seminary, where she received an education similar to the boys at nearby Union College in Schenectady, New York. While attending Troy, Elizabeth learned she was living in what historians called the Second Great Awakening, characterized by evangelical ministers proclaiming human sinfulness and a vengeful God to those who did not accept Jesus as Lord and Savior. Like their predecessors in the 1730s and 1740s, these radical and patriarchal leaders' interpretation of the Bible proved to be a great influence in Elizabeth's life, along with learning "how the law negatively affected women" [54] from her father's law practice. Stanton once said, "Nothing strengthens the judgment and quickens the conscience like individual responsibility," [55] something she found lacking in organized religion. She encouraged women to "do all you can, no matter what, to get people to think," [56] which is exactly what Stanton did—from serving as host of the first convention for women's civil and political rights in 1848 in Seneca Falls to writing many books and delivering speeches. Her writings included: "Declaration of Sentiments and Resolutions" (1848), "A Petition for Universal Suffrage" (1866), "Self-Government the Best Means of Self-Development" (1884), "The Degradation of Disenfranchisement"

Perhaps some day men will raise a tablet reading in letters of gold: All honor to women, the first disenfranchised class in history who, unaided by any political party, won enfranchisement by its own effort... and achieved the victory without the shedding of a drop of human blood. All honor to women of the world! [57]

Harriot Stanton Blatch
1856 – 1940

(1892), "Solitude of Self" (1892), "The Woman's Bible" volumes one and two (1895 and 1898), and "Eighty Years and More: Reminiscences 1815 – 1897" (1898).

Together with Susan B. Anthony, Stanton established *The Revolution* in 1868. The newspaper covered women's rights, politics, finance, the labor movement, and women's suffrage in a combative style to shock and grab their audience. They knew women wouldn't be given the right to vote; they'd have to fight for it. Their book *History of Woman Suffrage Volumes I-VI*, coauthored by Matilda Joslyn Gage and Ida Husted Harper, documented women's struggle. Anthony often stayed with Stanton to help with her seven children, giving Stanton needed peace to write.

On Stanton's last birthday, her eighty-seventh, Anthony wrote, "It is fifty-one years since first we met and we have been busy through every one of them, stirring up the world to recognize the rights of women…we little dreamed when we began this contest…[that] half a century later…another generation of women…[has] but one point to gain—the suffrage…." [58] Anthony's and Stanton's skills complemented each other in equal measure.

William Lloyd Garrison, abolitionist and women's rights advocate, characterized the suffrage pioneer by saying, "Mrs. Stanton is a fearless woman and goes for women's rights with all her soul." [59]

War Work

Woman's Loyal National League

1863

In January 1863, with the country almost two years into a civil war, President Lincoln issued the Emancipation Proclamation as a means to end the armed conflict. It granted freedom to slaves from states in rebellion if the Union won the war, which prompted hundreds of thousands of slaves to join the Union forces despite the fact that their freedom was not guaranteed by the Constitution post-war.

By then, the Women's Rights Movement had been fighting for fifteen years to convince men of women's equal status as citizens, and the war was dividing their supporters. Abolitionists saw the war as a chance to end slavery and claim full citizenship rights for black Americans. Women's rights supporters wanted to avoid any setbacks for their movement, as they had been gaining momentum since the Seneca Falls Convention and conventions in the years that followed. The first National Women's Rights Convention, organized by Lucy Stone, a prominent women's rights activist and anti-slavery advocate, took place in Worcester, Massachusetts, in 1850. (See chapter titled "Lucy Stone.") "Let woman's sphere be bounded only by her capacity,"[60] Stone stated the following year at the second annual Women's Rights convention, also in Worchester.

Elizabeth Cady Stanton, then a mother of six, felt that the importance of the war merited the cessation of the women's rights campaign, calculating that women's sacrifice for the war effort would be rewarded with their suffrage rights after the war. Susan B. Anthony disagreed. Through her prewar travels across the country giving anti-slavery and pro-women's rights speeches, she'd seen firsthand the country's hesitation to embrace women's rights. The volume of food flung at Anthony during her public speeches attested to the public's disapproval of a woman speaking in public and their objection to women attempting to branch into the men's realm. Stanton believed, "The policy of the war, our whole future life, depends on a universal, clearly defined idea of the end purpose, and the immense advantages to be secured to ourselves and all mankind, by its accomplishment."[61]

Anthony and Stanton, along with Lucy Stone, devised a compromise regarding women's war duties by forming the Women's Loyal National League (WLNL) in 1863 for the promotion of "the civil and political rights to all citizens of African descent and all women."[62] The inclusion of women's rights alongside blacks was controversial, but women knew they'd not obtain their rights alone. Anthony explained, "It is the simple assertion of the great fundamental truth of democracy that was proclaimed by our Revolutionary fathers."[63] With the help of two thousand volunteers, the WLNL collected one hundred thousand signatures from both men and women for "universal

We ask only for justice and equal rights—the right to vote, the right to our own earnings, equality before the law.[64]

Lucy Stone
1818 – 1893

emancipation" and had two free black men carry the large bundles into the U.S. Senate, where Massachusetts Senator Charles Sumner presented them to the Congress. By August 1864, the League had submitted three hundred thousand more signatures in support of freedom for all. At that time, theirs was the largest petition drive in American history "and marked a continuation of the shift of women's activism from moral suasion to political action." [65]

In January 1865, the Thirteenth Amendment abolished slavery. It did not, however, reverse the 1857 *Dred Scott v. Sandford* Supreme Court ruling that declared no black person, free or slave, could be a citizen of the United States. The year after the war ended, Congress passed the Civil Rights Act of 1866, which was intended to define the nature of citizenship and to proclaim all citizens as equally protected by the U.S. government. The act fell short and merely defined "citizen" by race and color, with no mention of sex.

Susan B. Anthony's forecast was correct: Women's emancipation was not included in the Thirteenth Amendment, nor was their right to vote. The Civil War ended in April 1865, but Anthony's years of traveling and campaigning for women's rights had to continue. Elizabeth Cady Stanton wrote many of Anthony's speeches and said of their writing/speaking partnership, "I forged the thunderbolts, and she fired them ... [Stanton's] husband put it differently, 'You stir up Susan, and she stirs the world.'" [66]

NO MAN IS GOOD ENOUGH TO GOVERN ANY WOMAN WITHOUT HER CONSENT.

SUSAN B. ANTHONY

Governance

American Equal Rights Association

To resolve the citizenship discrepancy of the Thirteenth Amendment, "birthright" was embraced by black activists as their measure for belonging and for the Fourteenth Amendment. Women supported this idea as an avenue toward *their* goal of winning the vote, though they knew they'd have to continue publicizing their separate message. Their right to vote was the one right women would relentlessly pursue despite it being the "one [right] man [would] most reluctantly give up," [67] Elizabeth Cady Stanton wrote.

Toward that end, Anthony and Stanton established a weekly newspaper, *The Revolution*, in January 1868 with the motto, "Principle, Not Policy: Justice, Not Favors." Its run lasted only four years due to funding issues, but the newspaper gave the two suffrage pioneers a broad platform to spread their ideas about women's rights and inclusion as equal citizens in the next Constitutional amendment.

On July 28, 1868, the Fourteenth Amendment became law, granting citizenship to "all persons born or naturalized in the United States." This legally resolved the issue in the *Dred Scott v. Sandford* Supreme Court ruling though many states subsequently passed laws that subverted the amendment's enforcement. The Fourteenth Amendment also included the word "male" three times, the first mention of sex in the Constitution. Women were not mentioned. Stanton and Anthony opposed the amendment for its omission of race and sex, but Lucy Stone supported it as a step toward universal suffrage, which was a continuation of her 1846 pledge that she wrote about to her mother, "I expect to plead not for the slave only, but for suffering humanity everywhere. Especially do I mean to labor for the elevation of my sex." [68]

The questions remained: Were women citizens, and as such, could they legally cast a ballot? In the same year as the Civil Rights Act of 1866, the women's movement reemerged with the eleventh National Women's Rights Convention, which created the American Equal Rights Association (AERA). The organization's purpose was "to secure Equal Rights to all American citizens, especially the right of suffrage, irrespective of race, color or sex." [69] Lucretia Mott served as president. Other notable members included Elizabeth Cady Stanton, Susan B. Anthony, Lucy Stone, and Frederick Douglass. Following three years of campaigning for the suffrage rights of blacks *and* women, the AERA's former abolitionist allies grew increasingly resistant to women's suffrage, viewing it as an impediment to their immediate goal of suffrage for black men via the Fifteenth Amendment.

Stone supported this strategy of separating causes, whereas Anthony and Stanton objected to it, arguing there was no need to focus on only one group of disenfranchised citizens.

Let women issue a declaration of independence sexually, and absolutely refuse to cohabit with men until they are acknowledged as equals in everything, and the victory would be won in a single week.[70]

Victoria Woodhull
1838 – 1927

They also worried the amendment would set a dangerous legal precedent of male superiority over women. Anthony and Stanton "sought to shock people into seeing the absurdity of excluding women from voting [but] their strategy often back-fired, depicting them as racially prejudiced rather than exposing the ridiculousness of gender prejudice."[71] Stanton was so infuriated by the Fifteenth Amendment, she said, "Think of Patrick and Sambo and Hans and Yung Tung who do not know the difference between a monarchy and a republic, who can not read the Declaration of Independence or Webster's spelling book, making laws for Lucretia Mott, Ernestine L. Rose, and Anna E. Dickinson."[72] Frederick Douglass, who supported the 1848 Women's Rights Convention, now argued the same point as "the Republican party [who] shouted back to [women], 'Keep silence, this is the negro's hour.'"[73] Stanton, however, believed, "We educated, virtuous White women are more worthy of the vote."[74] And though she and Anthony were opposed to slavery before the Civil War, their friendship with Douglass became strained postwar over the emphasis on black men's right to the ballot over women's same right. This prioritization of enfranchisement over the equal rights of all Americans to the ballot box created great tension between black and white communities. Stanton's racial rhetoric exacerbated the strain.

In April 1868, many women in the Boston area felt the AERA was too much a New York organization. Wealthy author Julia Ward Howe, who wrote the poem that was set to music and became "The Battle Hymn of the Republic," was among the women who started the New England Woman Suffrage Association. Howe became the association's first president, and Stone served on the executive committee.

The Fifteenth Amendment, which Congress passed on February 26, 1869, and ratified on February 3, 1870, declared the "right of citizenship of the United States to vote shall not be denied or abridged...on account of race, color, or previous condition of servitude," with no mention of sex, again excluding women.

Organize, Agitate, Educate
Must Be Our War Cry

Susan B. Anthony

Susan B. Anthony

1820 – 1906

"O, the crimes that are committed in the kitchens of this land!"[75] wrote Susan B. Anthony of the food she ate while traveling on behalf of women's rights. Frequently breakfast consisted of "bacon floating in grease, coffee without milk sweetened with sorghum, and bread, green with soda, while vegetables and fruit were seldom seen."[76] Her cross-country treks were a grueling, dirty business but necessary to spread the word across the growing nation that women could change their worlds. They deserved to be recognized as citizens with all the rights thereto. Of one train ride, Anthony wrote, "Any decent farmer's pigpen would be as clean as that car."[77]

Susan Brownell Anthony was born in Adams, Massachusetts, the second of seven children to Lucy Read Anthony and Daniel Anthony, an abolitionist and temperance advocate. In contrast to Stanton, Anthony was "tall and lean … [with] angular features."[78] She had brown eyes with one slightly askew, thick, straight, dark hair, and a serious mien. Her mother was raised Baptist but reared the children in her husband's Quaker community that "stressed education for both boys and girls, [and practiced] pacifism, and social justice … [They] wore plain clothes, used 'thou' and 'thy' in their speaking and writing, and did not dance, sing, attend parties, drink hard liquor, or marry a non-Quaker without permission"[79] from the Quaker community.

Education and curiosity were important to Anthony, and at seventeen years old, she attended a Quaker boarding school in Philadelphia. By age twenty-six, she was the headmistress of the female department of Canajoharie Academy in New York. Away from Quaker influence, she adopted more conventional speech and opted for more stylish attire. Her family moved to a farm outside Rochester, New York, which became the gathering place for local activists such as former slave Frederick Douglass, who became a life-long friend of Anthony.

The temperance movement was Susan B. Anthony's introduction to public speaking for women's rights. Drunkenness contributed significantly to women's abuse, for which they had no legal recourse. Anthony started the first women's temperance society and traveled, encouraging women to champion the important work of demanding their rights. She testified for the causes of women at numerous state and national legislative hearings throughout her adult life, educating lawmakers about the needs for legal change. The privileges of patriarchy proved a tough opponent, however. Men dismissed and minimized women's efforts for liberty. One example occurred on June 27, 1867, when Anthony addressed a hearing "before the New York Constitutional Convention with

Forget conventionalisms; forget what the world thinks of you stepping out of your place; think your best thoughts, speak your best words, work your best works, looking to your own conscience for approval.[80]

Susan B. Anthony
1820 – 1906

speeches and petitions for the recognition of women in the new constitution." Afterward, Horace Greeley, a former U.S. Congressman representing New York who did not fight in the Civil War, "said in his drawling monotone: 'Miss Anthony, you know the ballot and the bullet go together. If you vote, are you ready to fight?' Instantly she retorted: "Yes, Mr. Greeley, just as you fought in the late war—at the point of a goose-quill!"[81] Her quick wit often won the day.

"The prolonged slavery of woman is the darkest page in human history,"[82] Anthony once said. Though she was speaking about women's subjugation under a patriarchal society, she was likely not referring to the abuses suffered by black women under chattel ownership. That was an additional layer of women's suffering largely unaddressed by the suffrage movement, which was primarily focused on enfranchisement for "all" women as the vehicle to change other societal ills.

"We shall someday be heeded," said Anthony in 1894, "and when we shall have our amendment to the Constitution of the United States, everybody will think it was always so, just exactly as many young people think that all the privileges, all the freedom, all the enjoyments which woman now possesses always were hers. They have no idea of how every single inch of ground that she stands upon today has been gained by the hard work of some little handful of women of the past."[83]

Susan B. Anthony dedicated her life to agitating for women's civil rights. This encompassed a broad range of issues: abolition of slavery, education reform, labor reform, temperance, women's suffrage, women's marriage rights, equal opportunity, women's financial independence, and dress reform. She started numerous groups, local and national, to empower women to fight. She chose not to marry, despite offers, because she felt her role as women's advocate and wife/mother were not compatible. Of her many eloquent quotes, "Failure is impossible,"[84] is probably the most memorable. Anthony said this on her last birthday in 1906, and it became the watchword of the women's movement.

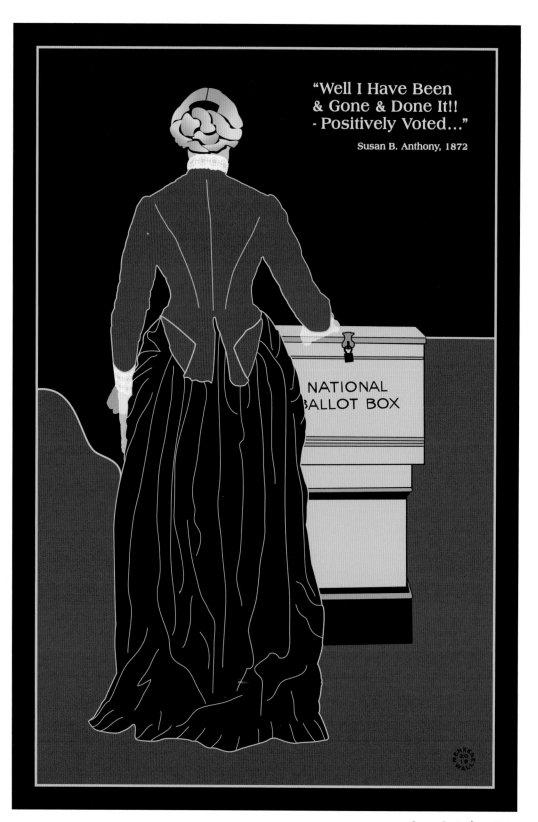

Susan B. Anthony Votes

Illegal Voting

The Thirteenth Amendment ended slavery, while the Fourteenth Amendment gave black men citizenship, and the Fifteenth Amendment conveyed upon them the right to vote. But the civil liberties of women continued to take a back seat to those of men. Anthony summed up women's determination this way, "We...solemnly vowed there should never be another season of silence until woman had the same rights everywhere on this green earth, as man." [85]

Susan B. Anthony and Elizabeth Cady Stanton founded the National Woman Suffrage Association (NWSA) May 15, 1869, to defeat the ratification of the proposed Fifteenth Amendment because its submitted wording made no provision for women's right of citizenship. That same year, Missouri suffragists Virginia Minor and her husband Francis, devised the New Departure, a strategy that argued the Fourteenth Amendment of the Constitution implicitly enfranchised women. As a result, hundreds of women attempted to vote. In 1871, NWSA officially adopted the New Departure and encouraged its members to attempt to vote; when turned away, they should sue in federal court with the defense of the Fourteenth Amendment that guarantees, "No State shall make or enforce any law which shall abridge the privileges or immunities of citizens of the United States."

On November 1, 1872, Susan B. Anthony, along with her three sisters, tested the amendment's citizenship clause when registering to vote in the presidential election. They demanded to be registered to vote, quoting the Fourteenth Amendment as their justification. Anthony even threatened to sue the election inspector personally if he refused to register them. After she registered, Anthony gave an interview at a local newspaper as to what happened, then drew broad attention to women's suffrage by giving a speech titled "Is it a Crime for a U.S. Citizen to Vote?" [86] twenty-nine times throughout Monroe County, New York.

Before she voted, Anthony sought legal advice. Did the attorney believe women had the constitutional right to vote? After reviewing the documents she provided, he said, "I will protect you in that right to the best of my ability," [87] believing Anthony's claim to be valid. On Election Day, Tuesday, November 5, 1872, Anthony and fourteen other women cast their ballots at the poll. They were surprised they were not turned away. Afterward, Anthony wrote to Stanton, "Well, I have been & gone & done it. Positively voted the Republican ticket" [88] for Ulysses S. Grant. Nine days later though, all were arrested for voting "without having a lawful right to vote." [89] Each posted bail to be released from jail except Susan B. Anthony. She demanded a trial. The proceedings were to be held in the

There are whole precincts of voters in this country whose united intelligence does not equal that of one representative American Woman.[90]

Carrie Chapman Catt
1859 – 1947

same county where she gave her speech "Is it a Crime for a U.S. Citizen to Vote?"

In court, Anthony's attorney stated, "If this same act [voting] had been done by her brother, it would have been honorable. But having been done by a woman, it is said to be a crime…I believe this is the first instance in which a woman has been arraigned [accused] in a criminal court merely on account of her sex."[91] The judge, Ward Hunt, was a known opponent of women's suffrage and refused to allow Anthony to speak on her own behalf until the verdict was delivered. After both sides concluded their case's presentation, Hunt read his prepared judgment and directed the jury to find Anthony guilty. This denied her the right to a fair trial from the jury that was impaneled to hear the case and render the verdict. When Anthony's attorney requested to poll the jury, Ward denied him and rendered his verdict of guilty. He then asked Anthony if she had anything to say.

"Yes, your honor, I have many things to say; for in your ordered verdict of guilty, you have trampled underfoot every vital principle of our government. My natural rights, my civil rights, my political rights, my judicial rights, are all alike ignored. Robbed of the fundamental privilege of citizenship, I am degraded from the status of a citizen to that of a subject; and not only myself individually, but all of my sex, are, by your honor's verdict, doomed to political subjection under this, so-called, form of government."[92]

Ward fined Anthony one hundred dollars—when the average worker's annual income was less than $400.00, to which she replied, "I shall never pay a dollar of your unjust penalty,"[93] and she never did. Was Sojourner Truth correct when she predicted that women's rights would fade from the political realm once black men received the vote?

Founded 1890

NATIONAL AMERICAN WOMAN SUFFRAGE ASSOCIATION

Women Demand An Equal Voice.

Carrie Chapman Catt

United We Fight

NWSA + AWSA = NAWSA

In 1875, the United States Supreme Court ended the question of who could vote. Their unanimous ruling in *Minor v. Happersett* stated, "The Constitution of the United States does not confer the right of suffrage upon any one…." This meant that either individual states had to enfranchise women, or the federal government had to pass a Constitutional amendment thereto. Following the ratification of the Fifteenth Amendment in 1870, which gave black men the vote, Congress added no amendment to the Constitution for forty-three years.

The proposed Nineteenth Amendment, wherein women would finally win the right to vote, was the same as the Fifteenth Amendment, except the Nineteenth Amendment added the word "sex" as a provision by which a citizen's right to vote could not be denied. First introduced in 1878 as the Sargent Amendment, the legislation, also known as the Susan B. Anthony Amendment, sat in committee for nine years before the full Senate rejected it. Each year thereafter, senators introduced bills calling for the amendment, and each year it failed until 1919.

In April 1888, House Judiciary Resolution 159 proposed "extending the rights of suffrage to widows and spinsters who are property owners," but it never went any further.

The National Woman Suffrage Association (NWSA) focused on a constitutional amendment to achieve women's suffrage, along with other social changes for women. NWSA wanted to reshape society's view of women to that of equal members of society, just as Lucretia Mott had called for decades before. To attain this goal, they worked toward improvements in other areas of women's lives, such as granting property rights to married women and unionizing female workers. NWSA was female-led. Politically, they even supported author Victoria Woodhull as the first female candidate for president of the United States in 1872.

But this was too radical for many in the organization. Lucy Stone and Julia Ward Howe favored a more conservative strategy and formed the American Woman Suffrage Association (AWSA) in November 1869 to pursue a state-by-state campaign with the sole focus of women's right to vote. They believed this method would more easily achieve women's goal to vote. AWSA also allowed for both male and female leadership and membership. By 1870, Stone and her husband began publishing the *Woman's Journal* to voice the group's position. AWSA was the larger, better funded, and more popular organization of the two due to its moderate platform, but its presence was concentrated regionally. NWSA had a regional reach in New York where they were

Why is a woman to be treated differently? Woman suffrage will succeed, despite this miserable guerrilla opposition.[94]

Victoria Woodhull
1838 – 1927

based, but their emphasis was on a national presence, enhanced by Susan B. Anthony's extensive traveling and speaking engagements for women's suffrage. Though both organizations held annual conferences through the 1870s and '80s, both struggled to maintain momentum.

Over the years, many had worked to bring the two rival groups together. By 1889, Lucy Stone's daughter Alice Stone Blackwell led the successful effort to bring the groups' leaders together to formulate a reconciliation plan. In February 1890, both associations' members approved that plan to form one organization called the National American Woman Suffrage Association (NAWSA).

It is significant to note that NAWSA's conventions excluded black women. NAWSA was more focused on appeasing their southern members who were not interested in having the Fifteenth Amendment enforced in their states because it could potentially undermine their white supremacy. Passage of the Susan B. Anthony Amendment would require the Yea votes of many southern congressmen.

At that time, American society was deeply segregated. To help bridge the divide, Mary Church Terrell and Margaret Murray Washington, two nationally renowned leaders of the National Association of Colored Women, encouraged black women to support "temperance because of its potential for improving conditions for many in the black community and the goodwill such activism could elicit from the white community."[95] Society was undergoing changes, but white suffragists did not focus on the race issue between blacks and whites. Society at large did not support black American rights in any measure of equality, and white women suffragists did not see embracing black women as advantageous to their goal of enfranchisement for all women. For white suffragists, inclusion centered on sex not race. They saw it as a practicality of the times.

Make The World Better.

Lucy Stone

Lucy Stone

1818 – 1893

"A wife should no more take her husband's name than he should hers. My name is my identity and must not be lost,"[96] Lucy Stone said about the practice of women taking their husbands' names upon marriage. Stone was one of the country's leading suffragists, abolitionists, and lecturers. Though she did use her married name for the first year of her marriage, she changed it back to Lucy Stone as it was more in keeping with her life's purpose of equal rights.

Stone was thirty-six years old when she married Henry Browne Blackwell in 1855. As a younger woman, she did not think marriage suited her independent nature since marriage, in the early-to-mid-nineteenth century, meant a woman was to give up her individuality to become identified by her husband's life. But Blackwell supported his wife's views, and they started their life together by omitting the word "obey" from their marriage vows and had a marriage protest read aloud at the ceremony and published in newspapers. In it, the couple proclaimed "the wife as an independent, rational being" and saw the laws that gave all powers to the husband as "injurious and unnatural." Some of those powers were "custody of the wife's person…exclusive control of their children…sole ownership of all property…[and] the whole system by which 'the legal existence of the wife is suspended during marriage.'"[97] At the time, "it became fashionable among other women's rights activists…to include their maiden names,"[98] such as Elizabeth Cady Stanton. Stone, however, was the first to publicly keep only her birth name.

Stone was born in rural Massachusetts, one of nine children born to Hanna Matthews Stone and Francis Stone. The cultural norms of the time did not encourage girls' education, but Stone wanted more than society's norm. She yearned to be a public speaker, so she became a teacher at age sixteen and saved her money toward a college education. In 1843, she attended Oberlin College in Ohio. After she graduated in 1847, with the sponsorship of renowned abolitionist William Lloyd Garrison, Stone began speaking across the north for the American Anti-Slavery Society. This began her long and lucrative career as a public speaker. By the time of her wedding, she had saved six thousand dollars, when an average laborer earned about three hundred dollars per year.

Stone was adamant that women deserved equal rights. To help make this point, she returned the tax bill on her and Henry's first house unpaid with an explanation that she was unjustly taxed without the benefit of representation at the polls. In response, the city seized some of their household items and auctioned them off to pay the taxes.

Stone was friends with Susan B. Anthony and Elizabeth Cady Stanton, and each was

Justice is better than chivalry if we cannot have both. "

Alice Stone Blackwell
1857 – 1950

supportive of the other's work for abolition and women's rights until they split over differing views about the Fifteenth Amendment. They eventually made amends, but during their rift, Anthony, Stanton, Matilda Joslyn Gage, and Ida Husted Harper wrote the *History of Woman Suffrage,* in which they marginalized Stone's contributions. Since their six-volume book was considered the standard scholarly text on women's suffrage for most of the twentieth century, Stone's achievements have been greatly overlooked.

Stone was driven by her zeal for speaking and traveled extensively throughout North America lecturing on women's rights and abolition. Often, though, her constant schedule brought on migraine headaches.

Among her many accomplishments, Stone organized the first national Women's Rights Convention in Worcester, Massachusetts. One of her speeches at that event was published in newspapers worldwide. She helped found the American Equal Rights Association (AERA), the American Woman Suffrage Association (AWSA), and the New England Woman Suffrage Association (NEWSA). Of Stone's weekly newspaper, Carrie Chapman Catt later said, "The suffrage success of to-day is not conceivable without the *Woman's Journal*'s part in it." [100]

Stone's daughter Alice Stone Blackwell also became a suffrage leader. When Lucy Stone was dying of stomach cancer, admirers wrote from around the world commenting on her "lifelong fidelity to one of the world's greatest needs—equal justice." [101] Just before she died, Stone whispered to her daughter, "Make the world better." [102]

The New Woman

Cycling Liberation

Forty-two years had passed since the Seneca Falls Convention, and women's lives continued to change, albeit slowly. The Victorian paradigm that identified woman by her domesticity and motherhood was shifting. "The New Woman" emerged—a term coined by writer Sarah Grand in her 1894 article "The New Aspect of the Woman Question,"[103] echoing Lucretia Mott's radicalism. Grand described women who eschewed convention and saw themselves as the equals of men.

Susan B. Anthony, now president of the newly formed NAWSA, noted society's progressive changes when she observed the correlation between the passage of decades and the gradual decrease in the volume of food hurled at her when she gave speeches. She was delighted to see how instrumental the bicycle was in moving women closer to the reality of equality by freeing them from lives of limitation. Elizabeth Cady Stanton commented, "Woman is riding to suffrage on a bicycle."[104]

The first bicycles were built for men, mostly as a toy, "another machine added to the long list of devices they knew in their work and play,"[105] said *Munsey's Magazine*. The original bicycles were wooden, with no chains, brakes, or pedals. Riders simply pushed off the ground with their feet. The next iteration added pedals to the front wheel. After a few other experiments and design changes, the basic bicycle shape used today came into being.

This mechanical agent of change necessitated dress reform, calling for more practical, looser attire with the return of bloomers from their introduction in the 1850s, which allowed for more physical activity. Bicycles proffered self-reliance to women as never before—to go where they chose, when they desired, and by themselves if necessary. These were all radical concepts in the 1890s.

Bicycles were affordable. This meant women of all classes and races could join in, not only the wealthy or the white. Black women also took to "the Wheel," as bicycles were called at the time. In 1893, a professional biracial seamstress and "a keen cyclist and racer from Boston named Kittie Knox joined the nearly all-white, all-male League of American Wheelmen"[106] at only twenty-one years old. The following year, she fashioned a gray knickerbocker suit for herself like the typical men's baggy trousers worn in cycling and won a July 4th contest at the Waltham Cycle Park, in Waltham, Massachusetts. Then in 1895, she presented her membership card at the league's annual meeting and made history. The league met in a socially segregated space—the Asbury Park hotel district. In 1894, the league had passed a new rule that "none but white persons can become members of the league,"[107] drawing into question Knox's right to participate. But her Riverside Cycling Club, Boston's only colored

Our opinion of people depends less upon what we see in them, than upon what they make us see in ourselves.[108]

Sarah Grand
1854 – 1943

cycling club, rallied behind Knox, explaining that she was a member prior to the rule change. Knox got on her bike and "calmly asserted her right to be there." [109]

Knox made headlines across the country, from the *New York Times* to the *San Francisco Call* with conflicting accounts of the incident. Some papers claimed she was turned away, while others reported her acceptance. Like all other aspects of black life, discrimination was ever-present, but Knox faced it and brought this instance of bigotry into public awareness.

"To women, [the bicycle] was a steed which they rode into a new world," [110] wrote *Munsey Magazine.* But her riding the Wheel embodied too much female freedom for most men to easily accept. Doctors, who were predominantly men, warned of a terrifying medical condition called "bicycle face," which was characterized by drawn lips, dark shadows under the eyes, and an expression of weariness. Some implied it could be a permanent state, while others maintained that, given enough time away from the contraption, "bicycle face" would eventually subside. To help women deal with such nonsense, author Maria E. Ward, an ardent bicyclist and cofounder of the Staten Island Bicycling Club, wrote *Bicycling for Ladies* in 1896. It was a guide of roughly two hundred pages that empowered women to learn how to buy, ride, dress for, and maintain their own bicycles. Ward's cycling passion was most likely influenced by her mother, a calisthenics instructor. Her book's illustrations were inspired by the photography of the club's cofounder Alice Austen, an acclaimed photographer.

As further pushback to women venturing out of their acceptable realm via the bicycle, the *New York World* newspaper published a list of "41 Don'ts for Female Cyclists." Among them were, "Don't ask, 'What do you think of my bloomers?...Don't imagine everybody is looking at you...[and] Don't chew gum; exercise your jaws in private." The best advice was, "Don't scream if you meet a cow. If she sees you first, she will run." [111] The New Woman ignored this and other alarmist warnings about cycling. Instead, she focused on the important business of expanding her world.

Music again marked the significance of women's progress with tunes celebrating the bicycle and bloomers such as "The Bicycle Girl," and "Bloomer Brigade March," in addition to "Bloomer March." Several composers went even further to emphasize women's accompanying societal and political challenges with "Women's Resolution," and "Equality Before the Law." Others were "Daughters of Freedom! The Ballot Be Yours," and "American Citizens Who Cannot Vote."

Change was indeed happening, and women's embrace of the bicycle forever altered the public's perceptions of proper female behavior.

Tyranny & Power

The bicycle provided a terrific boost to women's morale. But for real change, the kind that would give women control over their own lives and choices, they needed the right to vote, and the patriarchy stood in their way. As a commentary on men's general dismissal of women, Stanton observed, "[I]n the American Revolution, in 1776, the first delicacy the men threw overboard in Boston harbor was the tea, woman's favorite beverage. The tobacco and whiskey, though heavily taxed, they clung to with the tenacity of the devil-fish." [112]

Men still did not consider women their equal, and as such, continued to exclude them from rights that would empower women to alter men's dominance. Further exacerbating women's inequality was the influx of immigrants, notably the men. Stanton warned, "We should not allow our country to be a dumping ground for the refuse population of the Old World." [113] Knowing that the new male citizens would have influence over women's enfranchisement, she advocated, "Congress should enact a law for 'educated suffrage.'" Stanton thought immigrants "should not become a part of our ruling power until they can read and write the English language intelligently and understand the principles of republican government."

But people in power don't give up their authority without a fight, and they can easily find justifications for the existence of power in their own hands, as many American men did by embracing the Bible as the source of their God-given right to reign supreme. Stanton felt strongly that women would never obtain the right to vote with this common religious practice in place, and she wasn't alone.

Lucretia Mott stated in her "Discourse On Woman" speech in 1849, "I have long wished to see woman occupying a more elevated position than that which custom for ages has allotted to her." [114] She encouraged the "free discussion" of women's changing roles in society warning, "Those only who are in the wrong dread discussion." Mott argued that the Bible supported women's rights and became adept at refuting the male-dominated interpretation. Sarah Moore Grimké's "Letter on the Equality of the Sexes" in 1838 also spoke to the falsehood of women's ordained subordination to men. Lucy Stone even learned Greek and Hebrew so she could read the original biblical texts to confirm for herself her disbelief in this common patriarchal practice.

Matilda Joslyn Gage, another women's rights pioneer and author, wrote, "Do not allow the Church or State to govern your thought or dictate your judgment." [115] In her book, *Woman, Church and State,* Gage argued against the prevailing Judeo-Christian beliefs

I ask no favor for my sex. All I ask of our brethren is that they take their feet off our necks.[116]

Sarah Moore Grimké
1792 – 1873

that women were the source of sin and sex was sinful. With a committee of twenty-five other women, Gage assisted Elizabeth Cady Stanton in publishing *The Woman's Bible* in 1895. Its commentary addressed the first five books of the Bible's Old Testament and sold out the 50,000 first edition copies within three months. The second volume, published in 1898, commented on the remaining books of the Bible. The intent of *The Woman's Bible* was to challenge the prevailing patriarchal interpretation of the Christian Bible for a more radical theology liberating women. "We cannot accept any code or creed that uniformly defrauds woman of all her natural rights,"[117] Stanton wrote.

The Woman's Bible was a controversial and popular best seller. Many younger suffragists denounced it for fear it would harm the movement's goal of obtaining women's right to vote. Susan B. Anthony was not in favor of publishing *The Woman's Bible* until women first won their right to vote. She was concerned it would alienate religious men whose votes were necessary for a constitutional amendment enfranchising women. Still, Anthony defended Stanton as having "the right of individual opinion."[118] *The Woman's Bible* did not advocate for the rights of black women, which was the general practice within most white suffrage groups.

In 1896, black reformers founded the National Association of Colored Women with the motto "Lifting As We Climb." Not only did they fight for black women's suffrage but for the end of society's segregation practices: separate drinking fountains, schools, textbooks, and access to the polls. That same year, the U.S. Supreme Court upheld Jim Crow laws that enforced racial segregation, as long as the segregated facilities were "separate but equal." Throughout the struggle for women's suffrage, the "focus was on white-dominated suffrage organizations...at the expense of Black women suffragists."[119]

The Women's Political World newspaper, featured in the art for this chapter, was part of Harriot Stanton Blatch's efforts in 1913 to secure women's right to vote in New York State. As the daughter of Elizabeth Cady Stanton, Blatch worked tirelessly for women's rights. Four years later, New York State passed women's enfranchisement legislation in 1917.

Carrie Chapman Catt

Carrie Chapman Catt

In 1900, Susan B. Anthony stepped down from the leadership of NAWSA at age 80. She appointed Carrie Chapman Catt as her successor and Anna Howard Shaw as the vice president.

Catt, born Carrie Clinton Lane in Ripon, Wisconsin, was the middle child of Maria Clinton's and Lucius Lane's three children. When she was seven years old, the family moved to Iowa, and Catt aspired to become a doctor. Her father agreed to finance only part of the costs of college, so the enterprising young Catt worked various jobs to pay the balance—as a dishwasher, in the college library, and as a teacher.

Catt started her work for women's rights in college at Iowa Agricultural College, now Iowa State University. As one of six females in the freshman class of twenty-seven students, Catt advocated for women's rights to speak in male debates, subsequently started a girls' debate club, and joined the international women's fraternity, Pi Beta Phi. After she graduated as the only female in her class, Catt worked as a law clerk and schoolteacher. In 1885, she became the first female superintendent of Mason City, Iowa, schools. That year, she married newspaper editor and publisher Leo Chapman. He died the following year in San Francisco of typhoid fever. Catt moved back to Iowa and joined the Iowa Woman Suffrage Association.

In 1890, she married college classmate George W. Catt. That same year, and for the next two years, she served as Iowa Woman Suffrage Association's state organizer and recording secretary and began working nationally for the National Woman Suffrage Association where she was a speaker at their 1890 convention in Washington, D.C. Catt proved her mettle in 1893 by leading a successful suffrage referendum in Colorado, making that state the first to win the vote for women. The only other state where women could vote was Wyoming, starting in 1869 while still a territory, to attract women to the area. In the 1890s, when Elizabeth Cady Stanton was writing *The Woman's Bible*, Catt joined Anthony in expressing her concern over the book's radical tone and supported a NAWSA resolution that stated the organization "has no official connection with the so-called *Woman's Bible*." [120]

As president of NAWSA, Catt recognized the worldwide need to address women's suffrage issues, and in 1902, while serving as president of NAWSA, she started the International Woman Suffrage Alliance. Two years later, though, she resigned NAWSA's leadership to take care of her ailing husband. Anna Howard Shaw stepped up as president.

The death of Catt's second husband in 1905 left her a wealthy woman with the financial freedom to focus 100 percent of her energy on women's rights. She spent several years abroad

Woman is learning for herself that not self-sacrifice, but self-development, is her first duty in life; and this, not primarily for the sake of others but that she may become fully herself. [121]

Matilda Joslyn Gage
1826 – 1898

serving as president of the International Woman Suffrage Alliance while recovering from grief over her husband's death and those of her brother, mother, and mentor Susan B. Anthony.

In 1914, the attorney for the one of the richest women in America, Miriam Follin Peacock Squier Leslie, called Catt to inform her that his client, the owner of *Frank Leslie's Illustrated Newspaper*, had named Catt the major beneficiary of Leslie's estate, which was "valued at $2 million" [122] at a time when the salary of a member of Congress was approximately $8,000 per year. Leslie's instruction to Catt was to use the money for the women's suffrage cause. The news did not come without its challengers. Catt spent years fighting others' claims to the inheritance, spending "almost half of the estate ... on legal fees and settlements." [123] But the infusion of so much money excited many in NAWSA with one leader observing, "For the first time our goal looked possible of attainment in the near future." [124] By 1915, Catt helped found the Woman's Peace Party and resumed her duties as NAWSA's president.

Catt was responsible for implementing the "Society Plan" to recruit wealthy women with the time, money, and connections to help grow the suffrage movement. The plan's narrowed scope did not encompass working-class and lower class white women or black women. It also popularized a redacted version of the suffrage movement's history in the hope of gaining broader support. Members' involvement in controversial issues such as working women's rights, divorce reform, and racial equality were no longer discussed. Susan B. Anthony was lauded as the movement's saint, while Stanton's role as a suffrage pioneer was minimized due to her scathing critiques of organized religions in *The Woman's Bible*. Black women were not dissuaded by their marginalization, however. Many instrumental black leaders continued to fight for suffrage and black women's rights, including Mary Church Terrell, Anna Julia Cooper, Ida Gibbs Hunt, Ida B. Wells, Frances Harper, Nannie Helen Burroughs, and Mary Burnett Talbert.

Like all great leaders, Catt was imperfect, but she was a brilliant speaker and dynamic organizer with a magnetic personality. She worked for "The Cause" most of her adult life and came to be known as The Chief. In 1916, she delivered a speech in Atlantic City titled "The Crisis." It was a pep talk to encourage suffragists that they would indeed "secure [their] aim." [125] She punctuated the address with her now-famous line, "The woman's hour has struck." [126] Catt also formulated the "Winning Plan," which called for a coordinated state suffrage strategy to build consensus toward a national constitutional amendment for women's enfranchisement.

Among her many achievements, Catt founded the League of Women Voters in February 1920, which continues its significant work for women's rights today.

Men for Women's Suffrage

Men for Women's Suffrage

1908

Frederick Douglass, the former slave and prominent abolitionist, was an early supporter of women's suffrage. The day after the Seneca Falls Convention, he published a column in his abolitionist newspaper, *The North Star*, which asserted, "Standing [in 1848] as we do upon the watch-tower of human freedom, we can not be deterred from an expression of our approbation of any movement, however humble, to improve and elevate the character of any member of the human family... in respect to political rights, we hold woman to be justly entitled to all we claim for man." [127] Other men also spoke out for women's suffrage in the nineteenth century, but it wasn't until the twentieth century that men in larger numbers voiced their collective support. In 1902, Henry Villard, the publisher of the *Post* and the *Nation*—and grandson of William Lloyd Garrison, the prominent abolitionist, journalist, suffragist, and social reformer—joined other male supporters for "An Evening with the New Man," an event at that year's NAWSA national convention. In one of the earliest headlines about men's support, *The Washington Post* wrote, "Men Champion Cause: Woman Suffragists Not Alone In Their Battle."

In 1908, Anna Howard Shaw, president of NAWSA, asked Villard to again speak to their convention. This time he proposed another idea. He gave Shaw a list of a hundred influential men whose names and civic importance would "impress the public and the legislators" [128] with their support of women's suffrage. It worked. By 1909, George Foster Peabody, a prominent banker and financier, served as the first president of the Men's League for Woman Suffrage (MLWS). Most of their initial members had suffragists in their families.

In May 1911, eighty-nine MLWS members marched in the second New York Women's Suffrage Day Parade down Fifth Avenue in support of women's suffrage, despite the taunts from ten-thousand spectators of "Sissies" and "Hold up your skirts, girls!" [129] At some point, "more men with pennants joined the original brave band... and swelled the trousered company to more than 100." [130]

Many men were apprehensive about damaging their reputations if they chose to openly support women's suffrage. In answer to their concerns, the league's mission statement acknowledged men's fears, and in doing so, grew their membership and expanded the league across the country. "There are many men who inwardly feel the justice of equal suffrage, but who are not ready to acknowledge it publicly, unless backed by numbers. There are other men who are not even ready to give the subject consideration until they see that a large number of men are willing to be counted in favor of it." [131] State leagues

Liberty for each, for all, and forever! [132]

William Lloyd Garrison
1805 – 1879

throughout the nation enrolled an impressive list of recruits: respected men from academia and finance, military and religious leaders, newspaper editors, former governors, judges, and influential businessmen.

In coordination with NAWSA, these men used their connections and influence to advance women's causes in areas outside women's reach. They lobbied politicians, served on committees to influence legislative maneuverings, raised campaign funds, and persuaded prestigious publications to run articles about the suffrage cause. W.E.B. DuBois, a well-known black civil rights activist and editor of the National Association for the Advancement of Colored People's (NAACP) monthly magazine, *The Crisis,* wrote in 1915, "Every argument for Negro suffrage is an argument for woman suffrage; every argument for woman suffrage is an argument for Negro suffrage. Both are great movements in democracy." [133]

Another men's group to support women's suffrage was the National Men's League (NML) started in 1912 by James Lees Laidlaw, a wealthy banker and member of the board of directors of what became Standard & Poor's. As one of the Big Three credit-rating agencies, Standard & Poor's is known for its stock market indices, including the S & P 500. Laidlaw's wife was a major New York state suffragist. That same year, the NML's membership numbered twenty thousand. They organized state branches around the country, and their members participated in several state campaigns.

Men ran the country, and men needed to influence their cohorts to embrace women's new role as equal citizens with voting rights.

The committee is composed of married and single gentlemen. The bachelors, with beco... ...have left the subje... ...married gentlem... ...it with... ...have befo... ...ried life... ...they are... ...ble... at... ...ti... ...be... st... ...ver... and... ...ave ther... ...bed they... ...'s draw... ...hat of a gen... present time with... ...ashion, one lady occupies three times as much space in the world as a gentleman. It has thus appeared to the married gentlemen of your committee ... that if there is an inequity of oppression in this case, the gentlemen are the sufferers.

New York State Senate Judiciary Committee Chairman Samuel J. Foote
February, 1856

Vote No

Anti-Suffrage

Change usually begets some resistance, and prior to the twentieth century, anti-suffrage sentiments dominated among both men *and* women. Most believed in "domestic feminism," women's complete freedom within the home with deference to men in all other social, financial, and political matters. "We acknowledge no inferiority to men," stated anti-suffrage women in an 1886 Minority Report to the United State Senate titled "Woman's Protest Against Woman Suffrage." The report went on to say, "We claim to have no less ability to perform the duties which God has imposed upon us than they have to perform those imposed upon them. We believe that God has wisely and well adapted each sex to the proper performance of the duties of each...We believe woman suffrage would relatively lessen the influence of the intelligent and true, and increase the influence of the ignorant and vicious." [134]

Local organized opposition to women's suffrage began in the 1860s with socially prominent women making up the leadership of most anti-suffrage groups. In Lancaster, Massachusetts, two hundred women petitioned the legislature in 1868 to withhold women's suffrage, stating that "the moral influence of women" [135] might be compromised. The Woman's Anti-Suffrage Association was formed in Washington, D.C. in about 1870, and the Massachusetts Association Opposed to the Further Extension of Suffrage was started in 1882.

Women opposed to female suffrage showed up almost everywhere pro-suffragists campaigned, seeking to maintain the status quo "because the ballot has not proven a cure-all for existing evils with men, and we find no reason to assume that it would be more effectual for women." [136] They distributed publications, organized events, and sponsored state campaigns. Anti-suffragists thought the "suffrage movement is a backward step in the progress of civilization, in that it seeks to efface natural differentiation of function, and to produce identity, instead of division of labor." [137]

The official stance of women against suffrage was that "the suffrage is not a question of right or of justice, but of policy and expediency." Their argument continued with, "Our present duties fill up the whole measure of our time and ability," [138] and women "now stand outside of politics." [139] They believed it was their "fathers, brothers, husbands and sons who represent us at the ballot-box. Our fathers and brothers love us. Our husbands are our choice, and one with us. Our sons are what we make them. We are content that they represent us in the corn-field, the battle-field, at the ballot-box and the jury-box, and we them, in the church, the school-room, at the fireside and at the cradle; believing

A gentleman opposed to [women's] enfranchisement once said to me, 'Women have never produced anything of any value to the world.' I told him the chief product of the women had been the men, and left it to him to decide whether the product was of any value.[140]

Anna Howard Shaw
1847 – 1919

our representation, even at the ballot-box, to be thus more full and impartial than it could possibly be, were all women allowed to vote." [141]

Many anti-suffragists believed so strongly that "political equality will deprive us of special privileges hitherto accorded to us by law," [142] that they increasingly lobbied legislators and spent significant time away from their domestic duties to campaign for their cause.

Near the turn of the twentieth century, anti-suffragists started publishing a periodical, *The Remonstrance* (1890 – 1913), which promoted the movement's shared belief that "the great majority of their sex do not want the ballot, and that to force it upon them would not only be an injustice to women, but would lessen their influence for good." [143] Another publication was *The Woman's Protest* (1912). It was reorganized as *Woman Patriot* and published from 1918 to 1932. "Suffrage is the demand of a minority of women," they proclaimed, "and the majority of women protest against it." [144]

The National Association Opposed to Woman Suffrage (NAOWS) formed in 1911 in New York and later moved their headquarters to Washington, D.C.

Carrie Chapman Catt astutely described the glacial pace of political change saying, "No written law has ever been more binding than unwritten custom supported by popular opinion." [145]

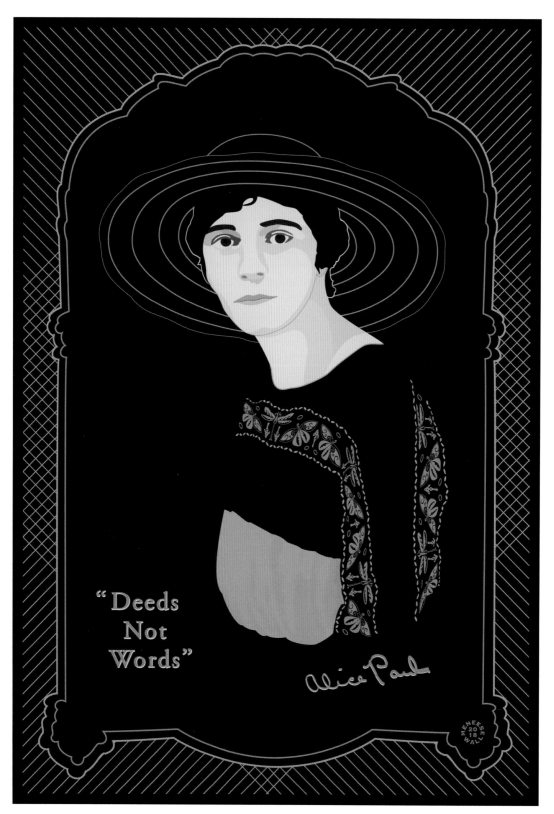

"Deeds Not Words"

Alice Paul

Alice Paul

Alice Paul

1885 – 1977

By 1906, the movement's pioneering leaders had died. Carrie Chapman Catt of the National American Woman Suffrage Association and Alice Paul of the Congressional Union for Woman Suffrage stepped up as the architects of the final push for a constitutional amendment for women's suffrage.

Alice Paul was reared on her family's 265-acre farm, Paulsdale, outside Mt. Laurel, New Jersey. They were Quakers, as were Lucretia Mott and Susan B. Anthony. Though Paul's parents were financially well off, they lived according to simple Quaker beliefs and practices of gender equality and the need to work for society's betterment. Alice's mother advised her daughter, "When you put your hand to the plow, you can't put it down until you get to the end of the row," [146] foreshadowing Paul's lifelong dedication to the cause of women's rights. Her mother was a member of NAWSA and often took young Alice to meetings.

After finishing first in her high school class in 1901, Paul attended Swarthmore College in Pennsylvania, which her grandfather, Joseph Wharton, cofounded with Lucretia Mott. A voracious reader, Paul earned both a master's degree and PhD. Between those achievements, she worked in the settlement movement in New York connecting the less fortunate with needed social services. This led her to a work-study program at the Quaker-based Woodbrooke Settlement in England in 1907. One day while out walking in London, Paul passed a loud crowd heckling a woman speaker named Christabel Pankhurst. Christabel was the daughter of Emmeline Pankhurst, England's most radical and militant suffragette—the British term for women seeking enfranchisement, whereas women in the United States were called suffragists. Paul introduced herself to the younger Pankhurst and subsequently joined their group, the Women's Social and Political Union (WSPU).

The movement's measures to attract public attention to the plight of women's social and political inequality were public and often violent, incorporating street speaking, heckling, window smashing, and rock throwing. Paul personally broke more than forty-eight windows. WSPU's motto was "Deeds Not Words."

While in a London police station, Paul met Lucy Burns, an American who was one of the WSPU's salaried organizers. The two had been arrested outside Parliament during a suffrage demonstration. In the course of their participation in WSPU, Paul and Burns were arrested and imprisoned several times for disorderly conduct. During their incarceration, Paul and the other suffragettes protested their confinement with hunger

It is unthinkable that a national government which represents women would ignore the issue of the right of all women to political freedom.[147]

Lucy Burns
1879 – 1966

strikes, the consequences of which were forced feedings. The women took solace in a quote etched on a prison wall, "Resistance to tyranny is obedience to God." [148] Thomas Jefferson expressed the sentiment, and later Susan B. Anthony adopted it for the American women's rights struggle. The British suffragettes' militant actions attracted London newspaper headlines with photographs of the police carrying the militants away in handcuffs.

In 1912, Paul began her involvement in the American suffrage movement by joining the National American Woman's Suffrage Association, which at the time had two million members. With permission from NAWSA, she and Lucy Burns formed the semi-autonomous Congressional Union for Woman Suffrage in 1913 to focus on the passage of a federal amendment for women's right to vote. The two groups eventually split over differences in tactics. Paul adopted more dramatic means similar to the Pankhurst's, though nonviolent, and NAWSA's approach was more conservative.

Paul was a brilliant political strategist and calculated that NAWSA's state-by-state campaign was too slow for women's benefit. She had an "enormous capacity for work" [149] and expected a lot of work out of her team as well. In 1916, the Congressional Union she and Burns created became the National Woman's Party, boasting fifty thousand members. The organization continues its work for women's rights today.

The Woman Voter

D.C. Parade in March

1913

Inspired by the Pankhursts' WSPU in London, Alice Paul believed women should not have to beg for their rights and set out to reshape and reinvigorate the American suffrage movement by raising public awareness of women's fight for enfranchisement. To accomplish this goal, she and Lucy Burns decided to stage a spectacular parade, building on the success of previous state parades whose largest crowds numbered twenty thousand. On Monday, March 3, 1913, Paul orchestrated the first national women's suffrage parade in Washington, D.C., the day before President Woodrow Wilson's first inauguration. It was a politically and symbolically powerful maneuver. Women would pass by great American landmarks like the U.S. Capitol and the White House while journalists from across the country could easily cover the pageantry, given they were already in town to report on the president-elect's big day. Paul strategized that the potential headlines would net broad coverage for women's struggle toward a federal amendment. Carrie Chapman Catt was not in favor of parades. She maintained, "We do not have to win sympathy [for our cause] by parading ourselves like the street cleaning department." [150]

That day, Woodrow Wilson expected throngs to meet his train at Union Station to extend a hero's welcome for his defeat of the sitting president, William Howard Taft, and former president Theodore Roosevelt who ran as a third-party candidate. His aide asked, "Where are all the people?" [151] Someone replied that they were watching the parade. Wilson was astonished. Though women had long agitated for the vote, the idea of women's suffrage was still widely unpopular.

The elaborate parade included thousands of women led by Inez Milholland. Like Paul and Burns, Milholland admired the Pankhursts' activism for women's rights in Britain. In college, she defied the school's ban on suffrage meetings by organizing them across the street from campus. Upon graduation from law school, Milholland advocated for the disenfranchised, including prison reform, garment workers' rights, and women's suffrage. She was a member of the NAACP, the Women's Trade Union League, the National Child Labor Committee, NAWSA, and the National Woman's Party for whom she was a popular speaker. She led the 1911 and 1912 parades in New York City and "snared suffrage more positive publicity than it had received in the past half century, thanks in no small part to media fascination with her Gibson girl good looks. 'No suffrage parade was complete without Inez Milholland,' the *New York Sun* contended." [152]

Atop a friend's white horse, Milholland escorted the parade as the "free woman of the future." Dressed in a white suit, gloves, and boots, with a pale blue cloak around her

I never doubted that equal rights was the right direction. Most reforms, most problems are complicated. But to me there is nothing complicated about ordinary equality.[153]

Alice Paul
1885 – 1977

shoulders and a gold star crown in her long dark hair, Milholland carried a trumpet "to herald the dawn of a new day of heroic endeavor for womanhood." [154] Behind her marched approximately eight thousand women from around the country and across the globe. The procession included floats, marching bands, banners, and regiments of women in white advancing down Pennsylvania Avenue, organized in matching costumes by countries, states, and professions. The Men's Suffrage League marched as well.

All participants were instructed "to march steadily in a dignified manner, and not to talk or nod or wave to anyone in the crowd." [155] The printed program stated, "We march today to give evidence to the world of our determination, that this simple act of justice [women's right to vote] shall be done." [156] The event "tied suffrage activism to America's long history of using parades to celebrate national values, implicitly wrapping participants in the flag ... This visual rhetoric lent moral authority to the spectacle of women marching in the streets, sending a message to [those] who opposed bold tactics." [157]

The event was not without controversy. Because Washington was segregated, Paul was concerned about alienating southern white suffragists. Her pragmatic solution, given the current political and social atmosphere, was to march black suffragists at the back of the parade. But Ida B. Wells, an outspoken advocate for black women's rights, refused that relegation and joined with the white Illinois delegation from her home state at the last minute "without incident." [158] The crowds of onlookers, estimated at five hundred thousand, refused to stand clear of the parading women. "The police protection that had been promised, failed them and a disgraceful scene followed ... Women were spit upon, slapped in the face, tripped up, pelted with burning cigar stubs, and insulted by jeers and obscene language too vile to print or repeat." [159] One hundred sixty-nine were arrested for obstructing traffic and more than two hundred were injured. "Through all the confusion and turmoil," noted an observer, "the women marched calmly, keeping a military formation as best they could."

The parade concluded with an allegorical tableau on the steps of the Treasury Building depicting the long road to women's voting rights. The multi-phase performance began with the parade's heralds playing a bugle fanfare. Fully robed women representing Liberty, Justice, Charity, Hope, and Peace, along with their attendants, then gracefully gathered around Columbia (the female personification of the United States of America) to dedicate this new "Crusade of Women."

Headlines proclaimed the parade and tableau a success. One headline read, "Parade Struggles To Victory Despite Disgraceful Scenes." [160] The movement was revived in spectacular fashion, resulting in women's suffrage taking central stage in the minds and on the lips of Americans coast to coast.

The Suffragist

WEEKLY PAPER OF THE
CONGRESSIONAL UNION FOR WOMAN SUFFRAGE

WINTER ISSUE

CREATED BY ALICE PAUL, 1913

IT IS UNJUST
TO DENY
WOMEN
A VOICE
IN THEIR
GOVERNMENT

ANY GREAT CHANGE MUST EXPECT OPPOSITION,
BECAUSE IT SHAKES THE VERY FOUNDATION OF PRIVILEGE.
Lucrétia Mott

MENEESE
20
17
WALL

The Suffragist

Newspapers & Magazines

To continue the momentum built by the success of the D.C. suffrage parade, the Congressional Union published a weekly newspaper, *The Suffragist*, launched on November 15, 1913. The publication was one of many creative tactics employed by the Congressional Union to further educate the public about women's political news and to garner more women's support for the cause.

Within its eight pages appeared announcements of upcoming events, volunteer opportunities, ways to give financial support, and articles about political maneuverings that could affect suffrage. To enhance the periodical's appeal and attract more readers, artist Nina Allender drew political cartoons that visually represented many struggles women faced in the fight for their equal enfranchisement. *The Suffragist* continued publication for almost seven years.

Suffragists published many other magazines and newspapers over the years to agitate for women's issues. Not long after the publication of Amelia Bloomer's *The Lily* in 1849, Paulina Kellogg Wright Davis launched *The Una* in February 1853 from Providence, Rhode Island, as a feminist periodical. Similar to *The Lily*, *The Una* was owned, written, and edited by women, but its sole focus was women's suffrage. Among its many notable correspondents were Elizabeth Peabody, an educator who embraced the importance of children's play to their development; Caroline H. Dall, a feminist writer; Fanny Fern, a novelist, children's writer, humorist, and newspaper columnist; Lucy Stone; and Elizabeth Cady Stanton.

Lucy Stone and her husband Henry Browne Blackwell published the *Woman's Journal* weekly, beginning in 1870. They soon incorporated two other papers, *The Agitator* and *Woman's Advocate*. Their contributors included Louisa May Alcott, a novelist best known for *Little Women;* William Lloyd Garrison, a prominent abolitionist, journalist, suffragist, and social reformer; Harriet Clisby, founder of the *Women's Education and Industrial Union* in Boston; and Zona Gale, an American novelist, short story writer, and playwright. In 1917, Carrie Chapman Catt used some of her inheritance from Miriam Leslie to found *The Woman Citizen* by merging the *Woman's Journal, National Suffrage News,* and *Woman Voter.*

Women's Tribune, a feminist newspaper founded by British-American suffragette Clara Bewisk Colby connected midwestern frontier women with the suffrage movement. Colby started the paper in 1883 in Beatrice, Nebraska, and moved three years later to Washington D.C. *Women's Tribune* ceased publication in 1909.

Character cannot be developed in ease and quiet. Only through experience of trial and suffering can the soul be strengthened, ambition inspired, and success achieved. [161]

Helen Keller
1880 – 1968

From 1909 to 1916, Charlotte Perkins Gilman published *The Fore-Runner*, a weekly magazine filled with progressive ideas to influence her readers. She performed every job: editor, book reviewer, journalist, essayist, poet, and storywriter with six serialized novels in the magazine. Her most notable serial was *Moving The Mountain,* a feminist utopian trilogy. She is best known for her short story, *The Yellow Wallpaper*, first published in *The New England Magazine* in January 1892. This short piece illustrated nineteenth-century attitudes toward mental and physical health and is considered an important early work of American feminist literature.

All of these periodicals shared one common attribute: They were written to serve white female Americans. But black Americans had their periodicals too, with most written for black communities as a whole, not just focused on black women's issues. Frederick Douglass published the *North Star* from 1847 to 1860, which focused primarily on abolition. His *Douglass Monthly* (1859 – 1863) expanded its articles to include issues on social reform. Other publications included *Frederick Douglass Paper* (1851 – 1860) and *National Era* (1870 – 1874). Notable periodicals included *Freedom's Journal* (1827 – 1829), a weekly New York City newspaper founded by Rev. John Wilk and other free black men; *Phillip Alexander Bell's Colored American* (1837 – 1841); and the *Christian Recorder* (1852 – present). Circulation was a challenge in black communities due to the illiteracy and poverty of many southern blacks. Freed northern blacks struggled to afford subscriptions due to low income, so they shared copies to help spread the word that they were not alone in their fight for equality.

In 1910, W.E.B. DuBois cofounded *The Crisis*, the official magazine of the National Association for the Advancement of Colored People (NAACP), with Oswald Garrison Villard, J. Max Barber, Charles Edward Russell, Kelly Miller, William Stanley Braithwaite, and Mary Dunlop Maclean. Its purpose was to expose "those facts and arguments which show the danger of race prejudice, particularly as manifested today toward colored people."[162] *The Crisis* continues publication today.

Josephine St. Pierre Ruffin cofounded *The Woman's Era* in Boston with her daughter Florida Ruffin Ridley and Maria Louise Baldwin, an educator, in 1892. It was the newspaper for their organization, the Women's Era Club, whose members were prominent black women devoted to addressing black women's issues, including suffrage. The paper was published monthly in Boston until 1894, when it started its national distribution until 1897.

Other periodicals in support of women's rights came and went, and all possessed an innovative, courageous spirit to bring attention to women's issues in times when women of all colors were expected to accept the status quo.

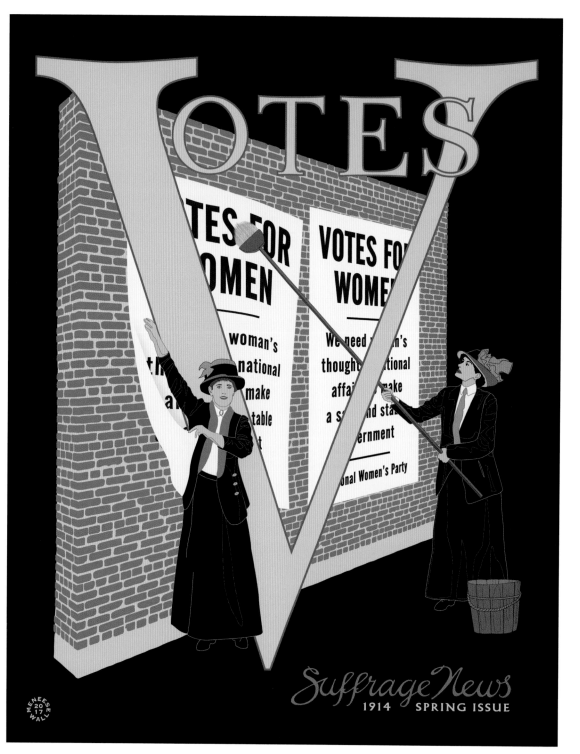

Public Propaganda

1914

In addition to parades, banners, pamphlets, newspapers, and magazines, suffragists gave talks to gatherings of all sizes and encouraged women to take action at home. Despite the fact that men believed women's place was in the home while men were to represent women in the public sphere, women had power. Lucy Stone encouraged domestic rebellion decades before women so publicly announced their intention to claim their power. She said, "When he says good morning, tell him you want to vote; when he asks what you are going to have for dinner, tell him you want to vote; and whatever he asks from the time you rise up in the morning until you lie down at night, tell him you want to vote." [163]

In 1914, the idea that women's sphere was restricted to the home persisted. Even President Wilson believed in this picture of womanhood, and with no women in either chamber of Congress, no one in government argued differently. However, the Constitution's First Amendment guaranteed free speech, and NAWSA and the Congressional Union—later the National Woman's Party—took full advantage.

Public displays in support of women's right to vote were certainly the most dramatic form of protest, and large posters pasted on buildings provided prominent longevity to the suffrage message. Newspapers and magazines announced upcoming gatherings and speeches and continually reminded all women that many people were willing to fight for women's rights. The posters displayed quiet encouragement to those in support of women's suffrage and those hesitant to publicly question the status quo.

Suffragists knew that tenacity and repetition would eventually lead to more women joining the cause, resulting in broader acceptance of eventual change. Decades earlier, suffrage pioneer Matilda Joslyn Gage said, "A rebel! How glorious the name sounds when applied to a woman. Oh, rebellious woman, to you the world looks in hope. Upon you has fallen the glorious task of bringing liberty to the earth and all the inhabitants thereof." [164] Women in the nineteen-teens rebelled more and more against society's limitations of women's social and political rights.

Alice Paul asked, "How is it that people fail to see our fight [for women's suffrage] as part of the great American struggle for democracy?" [165] Speaking for all women, she proclaimed, "We women of America tell you that America is not a democracy. Twenty million women [approximately half of the United States' population at the time] are denied the right to vote." [166]

The best protector any woman can have ... is courage.[167]

Elizabeth Cady Stanton
1815 – 1902

A growing number of composers contributed their talents to spreading the women's suffrage message with song titles such as "I'm a Suffragist" and "Woman's Suffrage Songs." The "Suffrage Marching Song" and "Votes for Hens" supported the suffragists, along with "Women, Women, Women" and "When Helen Casts Her Ballot." Women sang "A Suffrage Lullaby" to children to start them on the path of equal rights.

Suffrage News (1912–1920), featured in this chapter's artwork, was a local newspaper in Maryland aimed at applying pressure on the legislature to sympathize with women's issues and to serve as a source of suffrage news to women, because mainstream papers included almost nothing on the subject.

New World Order

Traveling Envoys

1915

Our nation's capitol and New York City were hubs for the women's suffrage campaign during its final push for a federal amendment enfranchising women. To garner national attention, women set out across the country to seek the support of women and men to achieve their goal. Two transcontinental automobile campaigns stood out: "The Golden Flyer," sponsored by the National American Woman Suffrage Association, traveled west out of New York, and the "Great Demand," sponsored by Alice Paul's Congressional Union, traveled east out of San Francisco.

"The Golden Flyer," with NAWSA's envoys Nell Richardson, Alice Burke, and their cat Saxon, traveled west from New York in April 1915 covering ten thousand miles with stops in New Orleans, Los Angeles, San Francisco, Seattle, Minneapolis, Chicago, Detroit, and numerous small towns in between. They gave speeches from their car and had people come to see the yellow two-seater automobile that had come to be a symbol of the woman's suffrage movement.

In September of the same year, the Congressional Union participated in the first Women Voters' Convention at the Panama-Pacific International Exposition in San Francisco. The exposition ran for ten months and drew an estimated nineteen million visitors. With the battle cry of "United!" their benefactor, Mrs. O.H.P Belmont, AKA Alva Smith Vanderbilt Belmont, summarized their mission in her opening address, "The women voters of the twelve enfranchised states...are met here to form a body politic... The western woman, with the power of her ballot [four million strong], will give to her enslaved sister justice and freedom."[168] Twenty million women, in the remaining thirty-six states, continued to be deprived of their right to vote. Appendix A shows when women could vote in each territory and state.

The convention concluded with a grand finale, a spectacular send-off of the "Great Demand"—two suffrage envoys, Sara Bard Field and Frances Jolliffe, on a cross-country auto campaign facilitated exclusively by women. Two Swedish women had just purchased a car and were planning to drive it back to Rhode Island, so driver Maria Kindberg and mechanic Ingeborg Kindstedt volunteered to drive the envoys to Washington D.C. with a banner displayed on the side of the car that read, " **WE DEMAND** an Amendment to the United States Constitution Enfranchising Women" *(emphasis added)*.[169]

Along the way, the envoys gave talks, handed out materials, staged parades and rallies, collected statements in support of their cause from congressmen in their home territories, and gathered pro-suffrage signatures on a petition to take to President Wilson and Congress

Pray to God. She will help you. [170]

Alva Smith Vanderbilt Belmont

1853 – 1933

for the opening day of the 1915–1916 Congressional session. The suffragists presented seventy-five thousand signatures on July 31st, to which twenty-three U.S. Senators voiced their support for a suffrage amendment on the senate floor that day.

These were not the first, nor were they the last, suffrage envoys dispatched from locations across the country to give talks in homes, schools, churches, and local theaters; hand out materials; encourage women to join forces to express their dissatisfaction with the status quo; and vote for the ouster of anti-suffrage officials in favor of politicians who supported women's rights. In many cases, they sold tickets to recoup their expenses and sent any additional money back to headquarters to further the cause.

Campaigns by car were difficult. Few paved roads and maps, in addition to no motels or restaurants between towns, scarce gas stations, and no air-conditioning made travel taxing. Add to that the requisite clothing fashions of the time—modesty from head to toe with only hands and faces free from cover, even in the heat of summer. Some envoys traveled cross-country by train as well. These campaigns, staged between 1914 and 1916, had a direct impact on increasing numbers of women gaining the right to vote at local and state levels. On the national level, Jeannette Rankin from Montana was the first woman member of Congress, elected in 1917.

Suffrage Bombs

Publicity Stunts

Following the tremendous success of the Washington, D.C. parade that revitalized the women's suffrage movement, NAWSA and the Congressional Union looked for other tactics to draw the public's attention to the cause of women's suffrage. Sixty-eight years had passed since the Women's Rights Convention in Seneca Falls, and bills for the Susan B. Anthony Amendment continued to fail in Congress. This time suffragists turned to the aeroplane to disseminate their message. They would drop "Suffrage Bombs" from planes onto crowds below.

It started with Rosalie Jones, or General Jones as she was dubbed by the press because of her army of suffrage followers, of the National American Woman Suffrage Association. In May 1913, Jones and her pilot climbed into a two-seater biplane and flew over a crowd of carnival-goers at an aeroplane show in Staten Island, New York. When the moment was right, Jones "bombed" the people below with yellow leaflets about women's suffrage. After landing, she gave a speech supporting suffrage and released a hundred brightly colored balloons.

Three years later, Lucy Burns, along with pilot Terah Tom Maroney, flew over Seattle to advertise the upcoming National Woman's Party convention in Chicago. Burns wore the suffrage cause's tri-colored sash: purple, the color of loyalty and steadfastness to the suffragist cause; white, the emblem of purity, symbolizing the quality of their purpose; and gold, the color of light and life, the torch that guides the suffragists' purpose, pure and unswerving. She brought along a suffrage banner to display on the side of the plane, but it quickly blew away in the 80 mph winds. Her suffrage "bombs," however, dropped successfully to the city below.

The most theatrical use of the suffrage bomb strategy was conducted in New York by two other NAWSA members, Mrs. John Blair and pilot Leda Richberg-Hornsby. The stunt involved President Wilson. The Great War had been waging in Europe for more than two years, and the United States had yet to officially join the conflict though it sent aid.

Train-car loads of dynamite and other explosives to help with the British and French war efforts were stored on the Black Tom peninsula close to the Statue of Liberty. On July 30, 1916, German saboteurs detonated the stash, killing seven people and causing minor damage in New York Harbor and to the Statue's torch and surrounding buildings. While the statue was closed for repairs, private donations funded installation of an exterior lighting system. That solved the statue's long-standing problem of virtual invisibility at night since its installation thirty years before.

Men and women are like right and left hands; it doesn't make sense not to use both. [171]

Jeannette Rankin
1880 – 1973

On December 2, President Wilson boarded his presidential yacht, *Mayflower*, anchored near Bedloe's Island and headed through the harbor to attend the lighting ceremony of the Statue of Liberty. While he sailed to the festivities, members of the New York branch of NAWSA gathered at a nearby airfield at 5:45 p.m. to cheer on their sisters Blair and Richberg-Hornsby. These intrepid suffragists boarded a two-seater plane and set out to "bomb" the president with yellow leaflets in support of the Susan B. Anthony Amendment, a provocative stunt that would make quite an impression for the suffrage cause. About a mile into the flight though, high winds made it clear this bombing would have to be aborted. The plane crash-landed in a swamp on Staten Island with neither suffragist sustaining serious injuries. They were, however, heartily disappointed to have failed in their mission to dramatically draw the president's and the public's attention to women's suffrage that day.

"This is war for woman's rights," said the pilot. "I am proud to fly for you."[172]

LIFTING AS WE CLIMB

Mary Church Terrell

Mary Church Terrell

1863 – 1954

Mollie Church, as she was known in her youth, learned at a young age to make the best of whatever situation she found herself in. She shared this philosophy of life through a story she told at her 1879 high school graduation, where she was the only black student. "Two monks were instructed to place peas in their shoes and walk to the next town. Upon arrival, one monk was in great pain, while the other suffered none. The distressed monk asked the other how he'd managed not to suffer, to which the first replied that he'd spent time boiling the peas prior to placing them in his shoes." Mollie called this her "boiling peas" principle and spent her life following its wisdom.

Mary Eliza Church was born on September 23, 1863, in Memphis, Tennessee—part of the South—during the Civil War. Her parents, former slaves, were staunch advocates of education and small business owners. Her mother was a hairstylist, and her father the South's first black millionaire. At age seven, Mollie was sent north to school in Ohio, where schools were not segregated.

After high school, Mary attended Oberlin College, "the first college in the country which was just, broad and benevolent enough to open its doors to negroes and to women on an equal footing with men,"[173] she later lauded. With a passion for languages, a degree in the classics, and a Master's in education, Mary landed her first job as a teacher of modern language at Wilberforce University in Ohio. Two years later, in 1887, she moved to Washington, D.C., nicknamed "the Colored Man's Paradise" because it was a gathering place for intellectual blacks. There, she taught in the Latin department at Washington's M Street High School, where her future husband, Robert Heberton Terrell, was principal. Following a couple of years abroad, where she honed her French and German, Mary Church returned to Washington and married in 1891.

Mary Church Terrell was no stranger to difficulties, but she "boiled peas" and accomplished a great deal. Her first three children died in infancy, though she later gave birth to her daughter Phyllis who lived to adulthood. She also adopted her brother's daughter Mary. In 1892, Terrell helped form the Colored Women's League with the goal of uniting colored women to improve their living conditions and education. In 1896, the league merged with the Federation of Afro-American Women to form the National Association of Colored Women (NACW). Terrell was named president and coined their motto, "Lifting As We Climb," encapsulating their mission to elevate black women within their communities, thereby advancing the entire black community. NACW's membership also included such important women as Harriet Tubman, Ida B. Wells, and

We are justified in believing that the success of this movement for equality of the sexes means more progress toward equality of the races.[174]

Josephine St. Pierre Ruffin
1842 – 1924

Fanny Coppin, a black missionary, educator, and advocate for female higher education. Terrell traveled widely, giving eloquent orations to black groups, encouraging them to embrace their race's achievements and potential, and to whites by dispelling the misinformation newspapers and common talk spread about black people being thieves, lazy, and untrustworthy.

In her 1898 speech "The Progress of Colored Women," Terrell addressed the National American Women's Suffrage Association, despite the fact that black women were not allowed to create NAWSA chapters. She acknowledged black and white women's struggles, their inequalities, and the work that lay ahead for both. "We look forward to a future large with promise and hope. Seeking no favors because of our color, nor patronage because of our needs, we knock at the bar of justice, asking an equal chance." [175]

From 1885 to 1901, Terrell served on the D.C. State Board of Education where she had the opportunity to give many more speeches. In 1904, she spoke at the International Congress of Women in Germany and delivered her speech in German, then French and English. By 1906, she was one of the most prominent black women in the country. She was a founding member of the National Association for the Advancement of Colored People (NAACP) in 1909 and fought for women's right to vote as well as for equality for all black citizens. In 1910, she helped found the National Association of College Women. Terrell marched in the 1913 Washington, D.C. parade, picketed the White House with her daughter, wrote and delivered numerous speeches including "What It Means to Be Colored in the Capital of the United States," published in *The Independent* (New York) on January 24, 1907, and wrote a book titled *A Colored Woman in a White World*.

Terrell applied to join the Washington, D.C. branch of the American Association of University Women in 1949, which caused a division in the membership because of her race. Ultimately, because of Terrell's affiliation, the group changed their bylaws to prevent race exclusions. In 1953, she won a lawsuit that ended legal segregation in Washington, D.C.

Mary Church Terrell was an icon for the advancement of colored people. She spent her life fighting for equality through education and social activism.

We Demand

Banners Not Guns

1917

Since the beginning of the Congressional Union in 1912, Alice Paul, Lucy Burns, and their volunteers relentlessly lobbied Congress for a constitutional amendment, as suffragists had done for decades. Following the example of the American Equal Rights Association during the Civil War, they also gathered signatures on petitions in support of resolutions and presented them to legislators. Petitions were tangible evidence of the people's support of an amendment for women's suffrage. Other promotional strategies included organizing large delegations of suffragists from various states to gather on the steps of the U.S. Capitol for protests and to later visit with their representatives. Suffragists also testified at Congressional hearings.

To keep tabs on every member of the House and Senate, the Congressional Union created a card index system. It detailed each legislator's background, including their public careers, pet projects, prior votes, and constituents' issues. With this information in hand, suffrage lobbyists could talk more persuasively with lawmakers. All of these tactics helped to shape legislative actions.

The Congressional Union also maintained the belief that the party in power, the Democrats, was responsible for women's inequality and their disenfranchisement—a key Pankhurst political strategy. NAWSA, however, supported President Wilson and sought members of the Democratic Party as their allies.

President Wilson wanted little to do with the women's suffrage issue. Starting in 1910, while serving his one term as governor of New Jersey, he anemically supported women's suffrage by saying, "I believe the time has come to extend the privilege and responsibility to the women of the State, but I shall vote…only upon my private conviction. I believe that it should be settled by the States and not by the National Government…."[176] Three years later, he was elected the twenty-eighth president of the United States. During his first term, Wilson was cordial to suffragists, holding occasional meetings with them, but he maintained the idea that women's suffrage was a state issue.

NAWSA supported the Great War in Europe (World War I), declared on July 28, 1914, by Austria-Hungary. However, Alice Paul and her suffragists in the Congressional Union did not. "When men are denied justice," Paul explained, "they go to war. This is our war, only we are fighting it with banners instead of guns."[177] Paul recalled the consequences of her predecessors' secession of their fight for women's rights during the Civil War. She knew Congress would not reward them with an amendment guaranteeing women's right to vote as a result of women's sacrifices supporting the Great War's effort. Paul determined

There never will be complete equality until women themselves help to make laws and elect lawmakers.[178]

Susan B. Anthony

1820 – 1906

that women had to maintain the fight and adopted a "votes-for-women-first"[179] policy, reasoning that they had to stay in the public eye or lose ground. From 1912 to 1916, Paul and Burns had waged their campaign on many fronts to no avail. They knew it was time to intensify their strategy.

So the Congressional Union, then forty thousand members strong, demonstrated with banners displaying phrases such as, "Forward Out of Darkness, Leave Behind the Night, Forward Out of Error, Forward into Light"[180] and "Without Extinction is Liberty, Without Retrograde is Equality."[181] Another banner read, "Resistance to tyranny is obedience to God."[182]

Soon their banners' rhetoric escalated. As their suffrage pioneer Susan B. Anthony had done, they quoted the Declaration of Independence with a banner that read "Governments Derive Their Just Powers From The Consent Of The Governed."[183] Two other banners quoted Anthony with "No Self Respecting Woman Should Wish Or Work For The Success Of A Party That Ignores Her Sex, Susan B. Anthony 1872 and 1874"[184] and "The Right Of Self Government For One Half Of Its People Is Of Far More Vital Consequence To The Nation Than Any Or All Other Questions. SBA 1878."[185] They also invoked President Abraham Lincoln with, "Lincoln stood for woman suffrage 60 years ago. Mr. President, you block the national suffrage amendment today. Why are you behind Lincoln?"[186]

Picket for Justice

Women Picket the White House

1917

While the suffragists' banners drew attention in the press, President Wilson retained his myopic focus on the war and his own re-election. During his presidential campaign in Chicago, the National Woman's Party (NWP) picketed with anti-Wilson banners outside the campaign's auditorium venue, withstanding mob violence during their demonstration. When the president was in Washington, D.C., he met occasionally with Carrie Chapman Catt of NAWSA to discuss women's enfranchisement. He respected Catt's counsel, as he resonated with her measured, non-combative style. Catt "remained convinced that the pickets' impropriety actively damaged suffrage chances...[and thought that] like black women in the 1913 procession [in D.C.], the pickets' visibility threatened the cause."[187] But the result of those meetings was always the same, no endorsement for women's rights. The president was merely placating the women to buy time for what he viewed as more pressing matters. On November 7, 1916, Wilson won a second term. The NWP continued to remind him of his obligation to all of America's people, not just the men.

By December 1916, suffragists' frustration was reaching fever pitch. Harriot Stanton Blatch told Wilson, "I have worked all my life for suffrage, and I am determined that I will never again stand in the street corners of a great city appealing to every Tom, Dick, and Harry for the right of self-government."[188] She agreed with Alice Paul that further pressure on the president was the path to follow. "We can't organize bigger and more influential deputations," Blatch explained. "We can't organize bigger processions. We can't, women, do anything more in that line. We have got to take a new departure."[189]

So that's what they did. The plan formulated during a December 25th memorial service for Inez Milholland, who had died in November of undiagnosed anemia while on a grueling suffrage speaking tour. "Blatch proposed a silent vigil, an unceasing picket line at the White House through Wilson's second inaugural in March... 'Let us stand beside the gateway where he must pass in and out...so that he can never fail to realize that there is tremendous earnestness and insistence back of this measure.'"[190] No one had ever dared to picket the White House, not even men; and many of the women were unsure of such an enormous step. That was until Wilson summarily dismissed a series of suffrage resolutions the women had passed while attending Milholland's memorial service and subsequently presented to the president.

The next day, January 10, 1917, a dozen resolute suffragists marched to the White House with banners that read, "Mr. President How Long Must Women Wait For Liberty?"[191] and "Mr. President What Will You Do For Woman Suffrage?"[192] They also carried flags

The old stiff minds must give way. The old selfish minds must go. Obstructive reactionaries must move on. The young are at the gates.[193]

Lavinia Dock
1858 – 1956

bearing the suffrage cause's tri-colors: purple, white, and gold. With few exceptions, such as black suffragist Mary Church Terrell, all picketers were white. At first, the president tipped his hat to the women, not knowing the proper protocol given that picketing the White House was a novel event. He even instructed the White House guards to offer coffee to the women. But these niceties didn't last long.

For the next few months, no matter the weather, several women took up their posts in front of the White House as Blatch's "Silent Sentinels," protesting the president's disregard for women's equal rights. Another banner read, "Mr. President: It is unjust to deny women a voice in their government when the government is conscripting their sons." [194]

Despite losing members who felt picketing during a war was unpatriotic, the National Woman's Party continued to escalate their banners' rhetoric. Among them was the tactic of pointing out the president's inconsistencies by using his own words to prove their point. From his war message to Congress on April 2, 1917, which explained his views for entering the United States into Europe's armed conflict, a suffrage banner quoted the president, "We shall fight for the things we have always held nearest our hearts—for democracy, for the right of those who submit to authority to have a voice in their own government." [195] Susan B. Anthony railed against this very kind of hypocrisy in her trial forty-four years earlier. One banner drew attention to Wilson's intransigence toward women's rights and social change by quoting Lavinia Dock, women's rights activist, nurse, and author of books on healthcare. That banner read: "The Young Are At The Gates." [196]

Wilson was more concerned with supporting democracy abroad than ensuring it for half of his own country's citizens at home. Suffragists weren't going to take it any longer, so their thought-provoking banners grew more and more incendiary.

Jailed For: "Obstructing Sidewalk Traffic"
Suffragists Go On Hunger Strike · Tortured With Force-Feedings

Night of Terror

Jailed in June

Many suffragists and new recruits bonded while picketing, thrilled by the teamwork and free speech aspect of the campaign to stand up against government repression. Their arms ached from holding the large pickets, however. Most were 10-feet-tall with banners that measured approximately 4' 6" by 5' 6", and they found the tedium of standing for long periods made their minds wander to "When will that woman come to relieve me?"[197] Across the ocean, Russia and Germany both denied citizenship rights to their people, and here at home, the National Woman's Party correlated that to women's rights in the U.S. with a banner deriding President Wilson as "Kaiser Wilson—Have you forgotten your sympathy with the poor Germans because they were not self-governed? 20,000,000 American women are not self-governed. Take the beam out of your own eye."[198]

Another banner quoted part of a speech by Wilson stating, "President Wilson—What Did You Mean When You Said: 'We have seen a good many singular things happen recently. We have been told that it is unpatriotic to criticize public action. Well, if it is, then there is a deep disgrace resting upon the origin of this nation. This nation originated in the sharpest sort of criticism...We have forgotten the very principal of our origin if we have forgotten how to object, how to resist, how to agitate, how to pull down and build up. Even to the extent of revolutionary practices if it be necessary to read just matters. I have forgotten my history if that be not true history.'"[199] Again the president's apparent cluelessness and hypocrisy galled suffragists.

Societal tensions were building—over the war and over women stepping outside their expected roles to voice opposition to their government in such a public manner as to embarrass the president. Though mob violence broke out a few times in association with women's picketing, it was the exception rather than the rule. The picketers remained quiet. Silent sentinels endured ridicule from people of all ages and sexes, who spat and made critical personal comments. It was when "the crowd would edge nearer and nearer, until there was but a foot of smothering, terror-fraught space between them"[200] that the women feared for their safety. A few banners were torn away by angry crowds and shredded to pieces.

On June 22nd, when the administration refused to change its position to support an amendment for women's suffrage, and when it couldn't bear the pressure of the women's civil disobedience in front of the White House any longer, the police started arresting women. By the end of the month, twenty-seven had been arrested for "causing a crowd to gather and thus obstructing traffic."[201] Two hundred eighteen women were arrested

I believe that the influence of woman will save the country before every other power.[202]

Lucy Stone
1818 – 1893

over the next four months, and one hundred sixty-eight of them were imprisoned. Why? To send the message to women to stop picketing. The suffragists had broken no laws. They were given the option to pay a twenty-five dollar fine or go to jail. They went to jail.

While incarcerated at Occoquan Workhouse in Virginia, the women were clubbed, beaten, and tortured with force-feedings. Alice Paul and Lucy Burns were arrested and force-fed numerous times. While in jail, Paul wrote to her mother, "I have been sentenced today to seven months imprisonment. Please do not worry. It will merely be a delightful rest." [203] Burns was manacled by her hands to the bars above her cell and forced to stand all night. Another woman suffered a heart attack and was denied medical care until the next morning. Paul demanded to be treated as a political prisoner, to which suffragists picketed with, "To Ask Freedom for women is not a crime. Suffrage Prisoners should not be treated as criminals." [204] November 14, 1917, was the worst night of abuse for the suffragists and so was dubbed the "Night of Terror."

"President Wilson had a public relations nightmare on his hands. At first, he (and almost everyone else) had dismissed the militant suffragists as crazed. But—with mob violence, so many arrests, and lengthy jail sentences—public opinion was shifting." [205] All were released on November 28th.

In March 1918, the D.C. Court of Appeals declared that all the suffragist arrests had been unconstitutional.

Ratification

Yellow Roses *vs. Red Roses*

1918

On June 7, 1918, President Woodrow Wilson wrote to Carrie Chapman Catt, "I welcome the opportunity to say that I agree without reservation that the full and sincere democratic reconstruction of the world for which we are striving [referring to World War I], and which we are determined to bring about at any cost, will not have been completely or adequately attained until women are admitted to the suffrage... The services of women during this supreme crisis of the world's history have been of the most single usefulness and distinction. The war could not have been fought without them, or its sacrifices endured. It is high time that some part of our debt of gratitude to [women] should be acknowledged and paid...." [206]

On September 30, 1918, after five years in office, Wilson delivered a speech to Congress changing his stance on a federal amendment for women's enfranchisement saying, "We have made partners of the women in this war... Shall we admit them only to a partnership of suffering and sacrifice and toil and not to a partnership of privilege and right?" [207] Suffragists finally won a powerful ally. To be sure, Alice Paul's militant techniques received more media coverage than Catt's negotiations. They spread the suffrage "Demand" message and influenced lawmakers. But it took both Catt's and Paul's divergent styles to convince the president of the political inevitability of women's suffrage as well as persuading him that he'd want to be remembered as the president who championed women's rights.

With the endorsement of the president of the United States, a federal amendment enfranchising women appeared poised to become law. The next day, October 1, 1918, the Senate took a vote on the bill with a bipartisan majority of senators supporting the proposal. But votes yielded a final decision of nay. The vote fell short by one vote of the two-thirds majority required for a constitutional amendment. The debate continued for the next three months. The unyielding Senators opposed to women's suffrage railed against the demands of the "petticoat brigade," while suffrage proponents said of their opponents, "Men are selfish, especially in the possession of power; they are loath to give up." [208] On January 10, 1919, the House of Representatives voted in favor of the Nineteenth (Anthony) Amendment, but the Senate fell short again in two separate votes over the next thirteen weeks. Wilson called a special session of Congress for another vote. This time, on May 21, 1919, the House voted in favor by a larger margin than before, and the Senate finally voted yea to approve the amendment on June 4th.

The final hurdle to the Nineteenth Amendment becoming a Constitutional amendment

The vote is the emblem of your equality, women of America, the guaranty of your liberty. That vote of yours has cost millions of dollars and the lives of thousands of women. Women have suffered agony of soul, which you never can comprehend, that you and your daughters might inherit political freedom. That vote is a power, a weapon of offense and defense, a prayer. Use it intelligently, conscientiously, prayerfully. Progress is calling you to make no pause. Act! [209]

Carrie Chapman Catt
1859 – 1947

was its ratification (acceptance and approval) by three-quarters of the then forty-eight states in the United States. Of the thirty-six votes needed, Wisconsin was the first to ratify the Nineteenth Amendment in June 1919, along with eight other states that month. Nine more states ratified by the end of September, and still five more by year's end. By March 1920, only one more state was needed.

In the ensuing months, eight states rejected the amendment, and five had yet to vote. Both Catt's NAWSA and Paul's NWP felt Tennessee was the most likely candidate for the thirty-sixth yes vote. "Suffragists called the battle for Tennessee 'Armageddon.'"[210]

The main battleground for the final ratification was in Tennessee's capitol, Nashville. Skirmishes were fought at the State House, the Heritage Hotel, restaurants, constituents' homes, and encounters on the street. Yellow roses of the pro-suffragists and red roses representing the anti-suffragists were the symbols deployed by the opposing sides in the fight for critical votes on the amendment. Music continued to mirror both sides' sentiments with pro-suffrage songs like "Equal Rights Rally" and "She's Good Enough To Be Your Baby's Mother And She's Good Enough To Vote With You." A funny title of note, "You Better Be Nice to Them Now" featured cover art depicting women in charge of various activities such as the office, building construction, and policing. Those opposed to the amendment could sing along to "The Anti-Suffrage Rose."

Carrie Chapman Catt directed NAWSA's strategy from her Heritage Hotel room. She and her team met with legislators and other influential people. NWP sent their chairman and Tennessee resident, Sue Shelton White, to head up their campaign. Alice Paul orchestrated her teams from her office in Washington, D.C. Josephine Anderson Pearson, president of the Tennessee State Association Opposed to Woman Suffrage and the Southern Woman's League for the Rejection of the Susan B. Anthony Amendment, headed the anti-suffrage efforts.

Summers in Tennessee are hot and muggy, and in 1920, there was no air conditioning to beat back the heat while the dress fashion of the day continued to be full coverage. Electric fans and cool drinks helped, but the heat of the issue at hand coupled with nature's temperature were enough to melt anyone's resolve. That didn't dissuade either side in their efforts to influence the legislature. For weeks, the negotiations and cajoling waged on with little ambivalence from either side.

Pro-suffragists had to fight against "a hasty coalition of anti-suffragists and upholders of states' rights, plus liquor and railroad interests who feared the woman voter."[211] On top of that, they feared "the threat of Negro domination."[212] Anti-suffragists often encouraged

*E*ducation and justice are democracy's
only life insurance.[213]

Nannie Helen Burroughs
1879 – 1961

legislators to cast the "correct" vote by leaving notes on their desks such as, "The men who vote against Ratification will go down in American history as the SAVIORS OF OUR FORM OF GOVERNMENT and the true Defenders of Womanhood, Motherhood, the Family and the State." [214] But Sue Shelton White had her team meeting with legislators 'round the clock as did Carrie Chapman Catt. During the debate to decide the matter, the state's former attorney general, General Charles Cates, spoke eloquently for ratification. "The men of Tennessee trust their honor to their women, and they should not hesitate to trust them with the ballot." [215]

On August 9th, Tennessee's governor, Albert H. Roberts, called a special session of the state's legislature to consider the matter. The amendment easily passed the state Senate, but the state House of Representatives was another matter. Nine more days passed before the amendment passed the House. Passage came only after a young state senator, Harry T. Burns of Niota, changed his vote from opposition to support, in concert with his mother's request. On August 18, 1920, Tennessee became the thirty-sixth and final state needed to ratify the Nineteenth Amendment.

Today we celebrate Women's Equality Day on August 26th because that is the day in 1920 that U.S. Secretary of State Bainbridge Colby signed the proclamation that certified the ratification of the Nineteenth (Anthony) Amendment.

Along the way, Alice Paul made a ratification flag in the suffrage movement's tri-colors and sewed on a new star each time a state ratified. She and many suffragists were elated to unfurl the final ratification flag in August 1920 at NWP's headquarters in Washington, D.C., with thirty-six stars affixed to it.

Equal Pay for Equal Work

Epilogue

Abigail Adams cautioned her husband, John Adams, the second President of the United States and cofounding father of our nation, "If women are not represented in this new republic, there will be another revolution."[216] She was right. Throughout women's seventy-two-year struggle to win their right to vote, they learned that they had untapped powers to demand their own liberties. And though the Nineteenth Amendment guaranteed all women the right to vote, in practice not all women were allowed to exercise that right. Black women, Native American women, Latina women, and Asian women were too often excluded from voting by state laws that legalized racial discrimination at the polls in violation of the Fourteenth, Fifteenth, and Nineteenth amendments to the United States Constitution.

In 1920, American society continued to be segregated. Jim Crow laws, the doctrine of "separate but equal," upheld by the Supreme Court in 1896, were legislated into law in former Confederate States after the Civil War. These practices allowed states to pass other laws more easily that severely restricted the voting rights of black citizens. Poll taxes, literacy requirements, state-sanctioned all-white primaries, and violence and intimidation were some of the tactics used by vigilante groups such as the Ku Klux Klan (KKK) to inhibit the minority vote. It wasn't until the Voting Rights Act of 1965, authorizing federal enforcement of voting right laws, that black Americans' enfranchisement was protected.

For Native Americans, their history of discrimination by the United States government has been long and egregious. Their lands were taken. Their children were forced to learn white ways of living, and they were marginalized onto reservations. They were not considered citizens nor were they allowed to vote. The U.S. government passed numerous laws to accomplish these atrocities including the 1830 Indian Removal Act, 1851 Indian Appropriations Act, 1862 Homestead Act, and the 1887 Dawes Act. Though the Fourteenth Amendment defined American "citizenship," it did not in practice include Native Americans, which meant they did not have access to the ballot. Not until the 1924 Indian Citizen Act were Native Americans granted full citizenship, but their right to vote had to be won state by state. Along the way, they were discriminated against at the polls through many of the same techniques used against other American minorities. Finally, by 1962, Native American enfranchisement was the law in all states.

Latinos experienced similar patterns of discriminatory voting rights practices. The law classified Latinos as white, but common practice excluded them from the ballot box

The first duty of a human being is to assume the right relationship to society—more briefly, to find your real job, and do it. [217]

Charlotte Perkins Gilman
1860 – 1935

through poll taxes, English-only ballots, and English-literacy tests. The right to have a jury of their peers also affected Latinos who did not receive jury summonses for decades.

In 1954 the Supreme Court unanimously ruled that the Fourteenth Amendment included all nationalities, positively affecting all minorities. In 1975 the Voting Rights Act was extended and amended to include minorities whose primary language was not English. This greatly increased Latinos' access to the polls.

Citizenship and the power to vote go hand in hand. Asian Americans, like blacks, Native Americans, and Latinos understood this all too well. In 1882, The Chinese Exclusion Act prevented certain Chinese laborers from immigrating and Chinese nationals from becoming United States citizens. In 1924 the act was amended to exclude all Chinese nationals as well as other Asian countries from immigrating to the United States. This meant Asians did not have access to the ballot to help shape laws that affected their communities. The Exclusion Act was repealed in 1943, giving Asians the opportunity to become naturalized citizens. Like Latinos and Native Americans, the language barrier was also an obstacle to Asians' access to the ballot box. The federal changes in voting laws of the 1960s and '70s gave Asians the access they were previously denied.

Today, women in America, regardless of their country of birth, can exercise their right to vote if they are American citizens, and they continue to fight for social, political, and income equality. As Susan B. Anthony said, "The day may be approaching when the whole world will recognize woman as the equal of man." [218] Until then, it's up to each of us to decide what we can do to "make the world better." [219] Voting is one civil right we can exercise toward this goal.

If there is no struggle there is no progress.[220]

Frederick Douglass
1818 – 1895

Acknowledgements

Writing and illustrating *We Demand The Right To Vote* showed me the power of history to change our lives, and at the same time it illuminated the boundless generosity of those who supported my vision. It started with Robert P.J. Cooney, Jr., Bob. Before we e-met, I was creating women's suffrage artwork, ascribing brief historical backgrounds to each, and selling them to anyone interested—well before the suffrage civil rights movement started to creep into the public's lexicon. I sent emails to everyone I could find who appeared to have any connection to this fascinating history. Bob wrote back. He described my work as "inspiring." Since that time, he has championed my creativity and shared critiques toward its betterment. His gentle, caring nature further energized my zeal to debunk the notion that women's contributions to history had been predominantly as wives, mothers, and domestic divas. His books on the subject are vital references to anyone studying women's history. I could not have imagined a more tenderhearted and steadfast mentor. Bob's review of my book warms my heart each time I read it.

Marianne Merola, my literary agent, was the fountainhead of *We Demand The Right To Vote*. Before knowing her, I wondered if anyone would be interested to include my artwork in a book on women's history, so I reached out to several agents. Marianne replied, "You don't need another author, you can write your own book." The thought never crossed my mind. A wave of imposter-syndrome washed over me. But with her veteran wisdom and ardent belief in the project, she patiently walked me through the process, critiqued initial iterations of my book, and guided me to the creation of the book's title. Marianne introduced me to a different view of myself and transformed my plans for the future.

As my knowledge of the women's suffrage movement grew, research led me to Coline Jenkins—the great-great-granddaughter of suffrage pioneer Elizabeth Cady Stanton. Coline is a film documentarian, author, and women's historian. Through her Elizabeth Cady Stanton Trust, she lends women's suffrage memorabilia to libraries, publishers, film producers, Congressional hearings, and museum exhibits to bring women's history into our present-day vocabulary. In addition to her warmth and positive attitude, Coline has shared my work with countless people, contributed a splendid blurb for *We Demand The Right To Vote*, provided research assistance, and encouraged me with her mantra, "Spreading the message of women's history is like throwing spaghetti against the wall. Do it; see what sticks; and repeat."

To manage the solitude of my writing and visual arts crafts, I wrote to authors whose suffrage books I'd read to share my vision and artwork while thanking them for their

The future belongs to those who believe in the beauty of their dreams.[221]

Eleanor Roosevelt
1884 – 1962

considerable contributions to my education. Many wrote back with lovely email replies, imbuing me with the solidarity of a subscriber to a club whose mission statement ennobled its members. I forged on with even greater resolve. Carol Lasser, author and Emerita Professor of History at Oberlin College, consulted on historical issues, providing further depth to my accounts of women's fight for the vote. Her counsel refined my view of *We Demand The Right To Vote* and challenged me toward an even higher ideal for its outcome. Elaine Weiss, journalist and author, inspired me with her detailed account of the final push for the Nineteenth Amendment's ratification. She generously applauded my work and contributed an eloquent blurb for my book.

Patricia Brown, Carly Mohler, and Brian Yee each buoyed my mind, body, and spirit throughout the creative process—Patricia with her sage wisdom, compassion, and counsel; Carly with acupuncture expertise and contagious zest for life; and Brian with craniosacral magic and restorative calm.

We Demand The Right To Vote was not complete until the writing was polished, and the visual presentation made alluring. Beth Crosby's discerning editorial prowess fine-tuned my voice with elegance and finesse. Through gentle nudges, outstanding commentaries, and pages of patience, she pointed my writing toward the engaging read I intended. Katerine Contreras collaborated with me on the book design. Her layout input refined my ideas into a visual work of art. Our shared insights into the importance of aesthetics polished my project masterfully.

Before, during, and after *We Demand The Right To Vote*, my family sustained me. My husband, Steve Wall, listened to my various artistic ambitions, ideas, and doubts with infinite patience. He advocated, advised, encouraged, edited, solved every imaginable electronic hiccup, believed in all my dreams—or faked it convincingly, and listened more. He is the yin to my yang and vice versa when needed. His curiosity inspires me, and his unwavering belief in me improves my creative endeavors and my life. Coco Wall, our daughter, is the catalyst for everything cool and current. She continually challenges me to see the world with an ever-progressive point of view. Her speed-reading research assistance helped immensely. They both enrich my life more than words can articulate.

To everyone mentioned here and to all who have enjoyed this book, namaste. When we look at our lives through the lens of the past, the present is better informed, and the future insightfully mapped.

Appendix A

Women's Suffrage Chronology

By the time the 19th Amendment was ratified in 1920, women in many states and territories already had the right to vote.

The following territories provided full voting rights to women before statehood:

    1869—Territory of Wyoming

    1870—Territory of Utah

    1883—Territory of Washington

    1887—Territory of Montana

    1913—Territory of Alaska

The following states granted women the right to vote prior to the 19th Amendment:

    1890—Wyoming

    1893—Colorado

    1896—Utah, Idaho

    1910—Washington

    1911—California

    1912—Arizona, Kansas, Oregon

    1914—Montana, Nevada

    1917—New York

    1918—Michigan, Oklahoma, South Dakota

In these states women could vote for President prior to the 19th Amendment:

    1913—Illinois

    1917—Nebraska, Ohio, Indiana, North Dakota, Rhode Island

    1919—Iowa, Maine, Minnesota, Missouri, Tennessee, Wisconsin

These states ratified the Nineteenth Amendment guaranteeing its passage into law (listed in order of ratification):

    Wisconsin, Illinois, Michigan, Kansas, Ohio, New York, Pennsylvania, Massachusetts, Texas, Iowa, Missouri, Arkansas, Montana, Nebraska, Minnesota, New Hampshire, Utah, California, Maine, North Dakota, South Dakota, Colorado, Kentucky, Rhode Island, Oregon, Indiana, Wyoming, Nevada, New Jersey, Idaho, Arizona, New Mexico, Oklahoma, West Virginia, Washington, and Tennessee

However, these states allowed women's suffrage only after passage of the Nineteenth Amendment:

    Alabama, Arkansas, Connecticut, Delaware, Florida, Georgia, Kentucky, Louisiana, Maryland, Massachusetts, Mississippi, New Hampshire, New Jersey, New Mexico, North Carolina, Pennsylvania, South Carolina, Texas, Vermont, Virginia, West Virginia

Appendix B

Referenced Amendments to the Constitution

Thirteenth Amendment

Section 1: Neither slavery nor involuntary servitude, except as a punishment for crime whereof the party shall have been duly convinced, shall exist within the United States, or any place subject to their jurisdiction.

Section 2: Congress shall have power to enforce this article by appropriate legislation.

Fourteenth Amendment

Section 1: All persons born or naturalized in the United States, and subject to the jurisdiction thereof, are citizens of the United States and of the State wherein they reside. No State shall make or enforce any law which shall abridge the privileges or immunities of citizens of the United States; nor shall any State deprive any person of life, liberty, or property, without due process of law; nor deny to any person within its jurisdiction the equal protection of the laws.

Section 2: Representatives shall be apportioned among the several States according to their respective numbers, counting the whole number of persons in each State, excluding Indians not taxed. But when the right to vote at any election for the choice of electors for President and Vice-President of the United States, Representatives in Congress, the Executive and Judicial officers of a State, or the members of the Legislature thereof, is denied to any of the male inhabitants of such State, being twenty-one years of age, and citizens of the United States, or in any way abridged, except for participation in rebellion, or other crime, the basis of representation therein shall be reduced in the proportion which the number of such male citizens shall bear to the whole number of male citizens twenty-one years of age in such State.

Section 3: No person shall be a Senator or Representative in Congress, or elector of President and Vice-President, or hold any office, civil or military, under the United States, or under any State, who, having previously taken an oath, as a member of Congress, or as an officer of the United States, or as a member of any State legislature, or as an executive or judicial officer of any State, to support the Constitution of the United States, shall have engaged in insurrection or rebellion against the same, or given aid or comfort to the enemies thereof. But Congress may by a vote of two-thirds of each House, remove such disability.

Section 4: The validity of the public debt of the United States, authorized by law, including debts incurred for payment of pensions and bounties for services in suppressing insurrection or rebellion, shall not be questioned. But neither the United States nor any State shall assume or pay any debt or obligation incurred in aid of insurrection or rebellion against the United States, or any claim for the loss or emancipation of any slave; but all such debts, obligations and claims shall be held illegal and void.

Section 5: The Congress shall have the power to enforce, by appropriate legislation, the provisions of this article.

Fifteenth Amendment

Section 1: The right of citizens of the United States to vote shall not be denied or abridged by the United States or by any State on account of race, color, or previous condition of servitude.

Section 2: The Congress shall have the power to enforce this article by appropriate legislation.

Nineteenth Amendment

The right of citizens of the United States to vote shall not be denied or abridged by the United States or by any State on account of sex.

Congress shall have power to enforce this article by appropriate legislation.

Notes

[1] Susan B. Anthony, *Letter to the Editor of the Chicago Tribune* (Chicago, IL: December 20, 1900).

[2] Joan Hoff, *Rights of Passage: The Past and Future of the ERA* (Bloomington: University Press, 1986), 8.

[3] Sandra Weber, "How Long Must Women Wait," The New York History Blog, Adirondack Almanack (October 27, 2016). https://newyorkalmanack.com/2016/10/sandra-weber-how-long-must-women-wait/.

[4] Ida Husted Harper, *The Life and Work of Susan B. Anthony Vol. I* (Indianapolis and Kansas: Bowen-Merrill, 1898), 169.

[5] Elizabeth Cady Stanton, Susan B. Anthony, Matilda Joslyn Gage, and Ida Hustad Harper, *History of Woman Suffrage Vol. II* (Rochester: Susan B. Anthony/Charles Mann printer, 1887), 631.

[6] Stanton, et al., *History Vol. II,* 631.

[7] Robin M. Chandler, *Women, War, and Violence: Personal Perspectives and Global Activism,* (New York: Palgrave MacMillian, 2010), 1.

[8] Stanton, Elizabeth Cady. *Eighty Years and More: Reminiscences 1857-1897.* (New York, Shocken Books, 1971), 83.

[9] Stanton, *Eighty Years,* 83.

[10] Stanton, *Eighty Years,* 83.

[11] Don Nardo, *The Split History of the Women's Suffrage Movement: Suffragists' Perspective,* (Compass Point Books, 2014), 7.

[12] Penny Colman, *Elizabeth Cady Stanton and Susan B. Anthony,* (Henry Holt, 2011), 47.

[13] Colman, *Stanton and Anthony,* 46.

[14] Elizabeth Cady Stanton, *Declaration of Rights and Sentiments.* Rochester, John Dick at the North Star Office, 1848, April 6, 2020. https://cdm16694.contentdm.oclc.org/digital/collection/p16694coll96/id/52.

[15] Stanton, et al., *History Vol. II,* 52.

[16] Martha E. Kendall, Failure is Impossible!: The History of American Women's Rights, (Minneapolis: Lerner Publications, 2001), 40.

[17] Colman, Stanton and Anthony, 46.

[18] Stanton, , et al., *History, Vol I,* 70.

[19] Stanton, , et al., *History, Vol I,* 71.

[20] Stanton, , et al., *History, Vol I,* 804.

[21] Judith Wellman, *The Road to Seneca Falls: Elizabeth Cady Stanton and the First Woman's Rights Convention,* (University of Illinois Press, 2004), 214.

[22] Mott, Lucretia, Lucy Stone, and National American Woman Suffrage Association Collection. *Discourse on Woman.* Philadelphia: T.B. Peterson, 1850. Pdf. https://www.loc.gov/item/09002748/.

[23] Carol Faulkner, *Lucretia Mott's Heresy* (Philadelphia: University of Pennsylvania Press, 2011), 2.

[24] Faulkner, *Heresy,* 2.

[25] Colman, *Stanton and Anthony*, 13.

[26] Faulkner, *Heresy*, 8.

[27] Faulkner, *Heresy*, 1.

[28] Mott, *Discourse*, 10.

[29] Mary Biggs, *Women's Words: The Columbia Book of Quotations by Women* (New York, Chichester, West Sussex: Columbia University Press, 1996), 189.

[30] Faulkner, *Heresy*, 25.

[31] Mott, *Discourse*, 4.

[32] Underwood, Benjamin Franklin, *The Free Religious Index Vol. I* New Series No. 5, (Boston) July 29, 1880, 245.

[33] Joseph Collins, "Lucretia Mott—Force for Equality," last modified January 6, 2017, http://infinitefire.org/info/lucretia-mott-force-for-equality/.

[34] Anne M. Todd, *Susan B. Anthony: Activist* (Women of Achievement), (Philadelphia: Chelsea House Publications, 2009), 33.

[35] Todd, *Activist*, 33.

[36] Harper, *The Life and Work of Susan B. Anthony, Vol. I*, 112.

[37] Harper, *The Life and Work of Susan B. Anthony, Vol. I*, 112.

[38] Harper, *The Life and Work of Susan B. Anthony, Vol. I*, 112.

[39] Amelia Jenks Bloomer and Anne Christine Coon, *Here Me Patiently: The Reform Speeches of Amelia Jenks Bloomer,* (Westport: Greenwood Press, 1994), 125.

[40] Stanton, *Eighty Years,* 163.

[41] Harper, The Life and Work, of Susan B. Anthony, Vol. I, 112.

[42] Frances Gage, "Sojourner Truth," *New York Independent*, April 23, 1863, 1. Voices of Democracy: The U.S. Oratory Project, Accessed August 8, 2019. https://voicesofdemocracy.umd.edu/truth-address-at-the-womans-rights-convention-textual-authentication/.

[43] Leslie Podell "Compare the Two Speeches," The Sojourner Truth Project, Accessed August 8, 2019, https://www.thesojournertruthproject.com/compare-the-speeches.

[44] "Compare the Two Speeches," The Sojourner Truth Project, accessed May 1, 2020, https://www.thesojournertruthproject.com/compare-the-speeches.

[45] Frost-Knappman, Elizabeth and Kathryn Cullen-Dupont, *Women's Suffrage In America: An Eyewitness History* (New York: Fact On File, 1992).

[46] Molefi Kete Asante and Abu S. Abarry, *African Intellectual Heritage* (Philadelphia: Temple University Press, 1996), 641.

[47] Carleton Mabee with Susan Mabee Newhouse, *Sojourner Truth: Slave, Prophet, Legend*, (New York and London: NYU Press, 1995), 173.

[48] Richard J. Douglass-Chin, *Preacher Woman Sings the Blues: The Autobiographies of Nineteenth-Century African American Evangelists*, (Columbia: University of Missouri Press, 2001), 64.

[49] Danilo Petranovic, Ralph Lerner, and Benjamin A. Kleinerman, *The Writings of Abraham Lincoln* (New Haven, Yale University Press, 2012), 81.

[50] D. Douglas Miller, Drumore Quakers' Precious Habitation, (Bloomington: Xlibris Publishing, 2016), 88.

[51] Colleen E. Kelly and Anna L Eblen, *Women Who Speak for Peace,* (Lanham, MD: Rowman & Littlefield, 2002), 30.

[52] Stanton, *Eighty Years*, 72-73.

[53] Stanton, *Eighty Years*, 21.

[54] Colman, *Stanton and Anthony*, 9.

[55] Valethia Watkins, PhD., J.D., "Votes for Women: Race, Gender, and W.E.B. DuBois's Advocacy of Woman Suffrage," Phylon: The Clark Atlanta University Review of Race and Culture, Vol. 53, No. 2, 2016, 6.

[56] Stanton, Theodore, and Harriot Stanton Blatch, eds., *Elizabeth Cady Stanton as Revealed in Her Letters, Diary, and Reminiscences, Vols. I & II,* (New York: Harper & Bros., 1922), 252.

[57] Karen Weekes, *Women Know Everything!: 3,241 Quips, Quotes, & Brilliant Remarks* (Philadelphia: Quirk Books, 2007), 418.

[58] Andrew Carroll, *Letters of a Nation: A Collection of Extraordinary American Letters,* (New York: Broadway Books, 1997), 183.

[59] Elisabeth Griffith, *In Her Own Right,* (New York: Oxford University Press, 1984), 73.

[60] "Proceedings of the Woman's Rights Convention held in Worcester, October 15 and 16, 1851", (New York: Fowler and Wells, 1852), 29.

[61] Robert P.J. Cooney, *Winning the Vote: The Triumph of the American Woman Suffrage Movement*, (Half Moon Bay, CA: American Graphic Press, 2005), 20.

[62] Stanton, et al., *History, Vol. II*, 5.

[63] Stanton, et al., *History, Vol. II*, 61.

[64] Stanton, et al., *History Vol. I,* 524.

[65] Wendy Hamand Venet, *Neither Ballots or Bullets: Women Abolitionists and The Civil War* (Charlottesville: University of Virginia Press, 1991), 148.

[66] Ellen Goodman and Patricia O'Brien, *I Know Just What You Mean: The Power of Friendship in Women's Lives,* (New York: Fireside, 2000), 188.

[67] Stanton, et al., *History, Vol. I,* 812.

[68] Karen Payne, *Between Ourselves: Letters Between Mothers and Daughters 1750-1982,* (Boston: Houghton Mifflin, 1984), 99.

[69] Stanton, et al., *History, Vol. II*, 171-172.

[70] Mary Gabriel, *Notorious Victoria: The Life of Victoria Woodhull, Uncensored* (Chapel Hill: Algonquin Books of Chapel Hill, 1998), 3.

[71] Sandra Weber, T*he Woman Suffrage Statue: A History of Adelaide Johnson's Portrait Monument to*

Lucretia Mott, Elizabeth Cady Stanton and Susan B. Anthony at the United States Capital, (Jefferson, NC: McFarland, 2016), 27.

[72] Carol Faulkner, *Heresy*, 195.

[73] Ida Husted Harper, *The Life and Work of Susan B. Anthony Vol. II*, 1016.

[74] Bettina Love, *We Want to Do More Than Survive: Abolitionist Teaching and the Pursuit of Educational Freedom*, (Boston: Beacon Press, 2019), 95.

[75] Harper, *The Life and Work of Susan B. Anthony, Vol. I*, 161.

[76] Stanton, *Eighty Years*, 248.

[77] Harper, *The Life and Work of Susan B. Anthony, Vol. I*, 242.

[78] Colman, *Stanton and Anthony*, 12.

[79] Colman, *Stanton and Anthony*, 13.

[80] Ida Husted Harper, *The Life and Work of Susan B. Anthony Vol. I*, 228.

[81] Harper, *The Life and Work of Susan B. Anthony, Vol. I*, 278.

[82] Stanton, et al., *History I*, Introduction.

[83] Lynn Sherr, *Failure Is Impossible: Susan B. Anthony In Her Own Words*, (New York, Time Books, 1995), xi.

[84] Ida Hustad Harper, *History of Woman Suffrage, Vol. V*, 1408.

[85] Stanton, et al., *History II*, 268.

[86] Harper, *The Life and Work of Susan B. Anthony, Vol. I*, 436.

[87] Harper, *The Life and Work of Susan B. Anthony, Vol. I*, 426.

[88] Stanton, et al., *History II*, 934.

[89] Harper, *The Life and Work of Susan B. Anthony, Vol. I*, 426.

[90] Elizabeth Cady Stanton, Susan B. Anthony, Matilda Joslyn Gage, and Ida Hustad Harper, *History of Woman Suffrage Vol. IV*, (Rochester, NY: Susan B. Anthony/Charles Mann printer, 1887), 371.

[91] Stanton, et al., *History II*, 632.

[92] Stanton, et al., *History II*, 640.

[93] Stanton, et al., *History II*, 644.

[94] Gabriel, *Notorious*, 112.

[95] Elna C. Green, *Southern Strategies: Southern Women and the Woman Suffrage Question*, (Chapel Hill: The University of North Carolina Press, 1997), 21.

[96] Sally G. McMillen, *Lucy Stone: An Unapologetic Life* (New York: Oxford University Press, 2015), cover.

[97] T. W. Higginson, "Marriage of Lucy Stone Under Protest," *The Liberator*, vol. 25, no. 18 (Whole no. 1085), (Boston), 71.

[98] Faulkner, *Heresy*, 3.

[99] Sheryl J. Grana, *Women and Justice* (Lanham, MD: Rowman & Littlefield , 2010), 34.

[100] Blackwell, Alice Stone. *Lucy Stone: Pioneer of Woman Suffragist*, (New York: Little, Brown, 1930), 243.

[101] Sally G. McMillen, *Lucy Stone*, 248.

[102] McMillen, *Lucy Stone*, 248.

[103] Carolyn Christensen Nelson, *The New Woman Reader: Fiction, Articles, Drama of the 1890s* (Broadview Press, 2001), 141. https://books.google.com/books?id=flLS5Lg9M_AC&p-g=PA141&dq=1894+Sarah+Grand%27s+article+The+New+Aspect+of+the+Woman+Ques-tion&hl=en&newbks=1&newbks_redir=0&sa=X&ved=2ahUKEwiN4aO39ZfoAhUBHcoKHe-hKBIsQ6AEwAHoECAMQAg#v=onepage&q=1894%20Sarah%20Grand's%20article%20The%20New%20Aspect%20of%20the%20Woman%20Question&f=false

[104] Christine Neejer, "Cycling and women's rights in the suffrage press." (2011). *Electronic Theses and Dissertations.* Paper 1047. https://doi.org/10.18297/etd/1047.

[105] Sue Macy, *Wheels Of Change: How Women Rode the Bicycle to Freedom* (With a Few Flat Tires Along The Way). Washington, D.C.: National Geographic Children's Books, Reprint Edition, February 7, 2017, 9.

[106] Joanna Scutts, "Women Cycling Groups Feminism History We Bike." Curbed, VOX Media, May 15, 2019 8:00am EDT. https://www.curbed.com/2019/5/15/18618037/women-cycling-groups-feminism-history-we-bike.

[107] Carolyn Szczepanski, Women's (Bike) History: Kittie Knox, The League of American Bicyclists. League of American Wheelmen, Inc. *dba* League of American Bicyclists, March 8, 2013. https://www.bikeleague.org/content/womens-bike-history-kittie-knox.

[108] Grand, Sarah. *Ideala: A Study From Life,* ed. Molly Youngkin (Kansas City: Valancourt Books, 2008), 211.

[109] Hilary Angus, "Three Women Who Changed the Course of History on Bicycles" momentum magazine. Momentum Magazine Ltd. March 5, 2015. https://momentummag.com/three-women-changed-course-history-bicycle/.

[110] Macy, 9.

[111] Maria Popova, "A List of Don'ts for Women on Bicycles Circa 1895," Brain Pickings. January 3, 2012. https://www.brainpickings.org/2012/01/03/donts-for-women-on-bicycles-1895/.

[112] Elizabeth Cady Stanton, *The Woman's Bible Vol.* 1, (New York: European Publishing, 1895), 40.

[113] Ida Husted Harper, *The Life and Work of Susan B. Anthony Vol. V* (Indianapolis and Kansas City: Bowen-Merrill, 1898), 32.

[114] Mott, *Discourse*, 1.

[115] Matilda Joslyn Gage, *Woman, Church and State* (Chicago: Charles H. Kerr, 1893), Introduction.

[116] Anna Russell, *So Here I Am: Speeches by Great Women to Empower and Inspire* (White Lion Publishing, 2019), 85.

[117] Elizabeth Cady Stanton, *The Woman's Bible Vol. I* (New York: European Publishing, 1895), 58.

[118] Harper, *The Life and Work of Susan B. Anthony, Vol. II*, 853.

[119] Watkins, *Votes*, 18.

[120] Harper, *The Life and Work of Susan B. Anthony, Vol II*, 853.

[121] Gage, *Woman, Church and State*, 531.

[122] Elaine Weiss, *The Woman's Hour: The Great Fight to Win the Vote* (New York: Viking, 2018), 194.

[123] Weiss, *The Woman's Hour*, 195.

[124] Jacqueline Van Voris, *Carrie Chapman Catt: A Public Life* (New York, The Feminist Press, City University of New York, 1987), 135.

[125] Carrie Chapman Catt, *"The Crisis"* Speech. New York, National American Woman Suffrage Association Convention, September 7, 1916. https://awpc.cattcenter.iastate.edu/2017/03/21/the-crisis-sept-7-1916/.

[126] Catt, *"The Crisis."*

[127] Stanton, et al., *History Vol. II*, 74-75.

[128] Brooke Kroeger, *The Suffragents: How Women Used Men to Get the Vote* (Albany: State University of New York, 2017), 11.

[129] Kroeger, *The Suffragents*, 3.

[130] Kroeger, *The Suffragents*, 77.

[131] Kroeger, *The Suffragents*, 102.

[132] Charles T. Sprading, *Liberty and the Great Libertarians,* (Los Angeles: Golden Press, 2015), 154.

[133] W.E.B. DuBois, "Woman Suffrage," The Modernist Journals Project (searchable database). Brown and Tulsa Universities, ongoing. www.modjourn.org/issue/bdr519604/, 285.

[134] Cooney, *Winning the Vote*, 51.

[135] Nancy Signorielli, *Women in Communication: A Biographical Sourcebook,* (Westport, Greenwood Press, 1996), 192.

[136] National Association Opposed To Woman Suffrage, 1.

[137] National Association Opposed To Woman Suffrage, 1.

[138] National Association Opposed To Woman Suffrage, 1.

[139] National Association Opposed To Woman Suffrage, 1.

[140] Stanton, et al., *History Vol. II*, 337.

[141] National Association Opposed To Woman Suffrage, 1.

[142] National Association Opposed To Woman Suffrage, 1.

[143] Jane Jerome Camhi, *Women Against Women: American Anti-Suffragism, 1880-1920,* (Carlson Publishing, 1994), 89.

[144] National Association Opposed To Woman Suffrage, 1.

[145] Stanton, et al., *History Vol. IV*, 370.

[146] Amelia Fry, "Audio Interview" Alice Paul Institute, May 12, 1973, http://www.alicepaul.org/audio-interview/. Via Erin, Sawadzki at Alice Paul Institute.

[147] Heather E. Schwartz, *Girls Rebel!: Amazing Tales of Women Who Broke the Mold* (North Mankato, MN; Capstone Press; 2015), 40.

[148] National Woman's Party, *The Suffragist* (Washington, D.C. January 10, 1917), cover page.

[149] J.D. Zahniser and Amelia R. Fry, *Alice Paul: Claiming Power* (New York: Oxford University Press, 2014), 131.

[150] Pamela Cobrin, *From Winning the Vote to Directing on Broadway: The Emergence of Women on the New York Stage, 1880-1927* (Newark: University of Delaware Press, 2009), 23.

[151] Michael Waldman, *The Fight To Vote*, (New York: Simon & Schuster, Feb. 23, 2016), 119.

[152] Linda J. Lumsden, *Inez: The Life and Times of Inez Milholland* (Bloomington & Indianapolis: Indiana University Press, 2016), 70.

[153] Carrie Fredericks, *Amendment XIX: Granting Women the Right to Vote* (New Haven: Greenhaven Press), 18.

[154] Cooney, *Winning the Vote*, 193.

[155] Zahniser and Fry, *Alice Paul*, 145.

[156] Zahniser and Fry, *Alice Paul*, 145.

[157] Zahniser and Fry, *Alice Paul*, 145.

[158] Zahniser and Fry, *Alice Paul*, 149.

[159] "Parade Struggles To Victory Despite Disgraceful Scenes," *Woman's Journal and Suffrage News* (Boston, MA), Vol. XLIV. No. 10, Saturday, March 8, 1913), 1.

[160] "Parade Struggles to Victory Despite Disgraceful Scenes," *Woman's Journal and Suffrage News*, vol. XLIV, no. 10, (Boston), March 8, 1913, 1.

[161] Kathleen A. Brehony, *After the Darkest Hour: How Suffering Begins the Journey to Wisdom*, (New York: Henry Holt, 2000), 13.

[162] David Levering Lewis, *W. E. B. Du Bois: Biography of a Race 1868–1919*. (New York: Henry Holt and Co., 1993), 312.

[163] Andrea Moore Kerr, *Lucy Stone: Speaking Out For Equality* (New Brunswick: Rutgers University Press, 1992), 158.

[164] Matilda Joslyn Gage, "Women Rebels." *The National Citizen and Ballot Box* (Syracuse), May 1880.

[165] Linda G. Ford, *Iron-Jawed Angels: The Suffrage Militancy of the National Woman's Party*, 1912-1920, (Lanham, MD; University Press of America; 1991), 189.

[166] National Woman's Party, *The Suffragist* (Washington D.C., June 23, 1917), 7.

[167] Stanton, et al., *History*, 816.

[168] National Woman's Party, *The Suffragist*, August 21, 1915, 5.

[169] Suffrage envoys from San Francisco greeted in New Jersey on their way to Washington to present a petition to Congress Suffrage envoys from San Francisco greeted containing more than 500,000 signatures. New Jersey United States, 1915. [Nov.-Dec] Photograph. https://www.loc.gov/item/mnwp000422/.

[170] Helen Rappaport, Encyclopedia of Women Social Reformers (Santa Barbara, ABC-CLIO, Inc., CA, 2001), 68.

[171] Karen L. Owen, *The Women Officeholders and the Role Models Who Pioneered the Way* (Lanham, MD:

Lexington Books, 2017), 43.

172 Maureen Maryanski, *The "Suff Bird Women" and Woodrow Wilson* (March 26, 2014, blog.NYHistory. org/the-suff-bird-women-and-woodrow-wilson.

173 Mary Church Terrell, Columbia Theatre, Daniel Murray Pamphlet Collection, and African American Pamphlet Collection. *The Progress of Colored Women*. [Washington, D.C., Smith Brothers, Printers, 1898] Pdf. Accessed on January 24, 2020. https://lccn.loc.gov/90898298, https://www.loc.gov/resource/lcrbmrp.t0a13/?sp=1&r=-0.516,-0.031,2.032,1.336,0, .

174 W.E.B. DuBois, *The Crisis Magazine*, Vol. 10 No. 1 Woman Suffrage (Editorial Woman Suffrage, May 1915), 188.

175 Terrell, "Progress".

176 Woodrow *Wilson, Wilson, Vol. IV: Confusions and Crises, 1915-1916,* (Princeton: Princeton University Press, 1964), 12.

177 "National Woman's Party Protests During World War I," National Park Service, Experience Your America™, May 15, 2019. https://www.nps.gov/articles/national-womans-party-protests-world-war-i. htm.

178 Feryal M. Cherif, *Myths about Women's Rights: How, Where, and Why Rights Advance* (New York: Oxford University Press, 2015), 87.

179 Inez Haynes Irwin, *The Story of Alice Paul and the National Woman's Party* (Denlinger's Publishers, Fairfax, Virginia, 1964, 1977), 42.

180 National Woman's Party, *The Suffragist*. 5.

181 National Woman's Party, *The Suffragist*. Textile Collection, Catalog #1913.033, 1913-1920. https://nationalwomansparty.pastperfectonline.com/webobject/1925C56F-9310-4E84-A67D-179389594096

182 National Woman's Party, *The Suffragist*, cover.

183 National Woman's Party, *The Suffragist*, 4.

184 Harper, T*he Life and Work of Susan B. Anthony, Vol. II*, (Indianapolis and Kansas City: Bowen-Merrill, 1898), 794.

185 Ann D. Gordon, *The Selected Papers of Elizabeth Cady Stanton and Susan B. Anthony Vol. III* (New Brunswick: Rutgers University Press, 2003), 404.

186 Harris & Ewing, Washington, D.C. *Lincoln's birthday. On the banners during Congressional debate on whether we should enter the war.* United States, 1917. Photograph. https://www.loc.gov/resource/mnwp160036/.

187 Zahniser and Fry, *Alice Paul*, 290.

188 Edwina Helton and Jeffrey Jones, *The American Suffragette's Journey to Enfranchisement: From Seneca Falls To Ratificaiton of the Nineteenth Amendment,* (Minnetonka, MN; Meadowbrook Publishing; 2018), 129.

189 Doris Stevens, *Jailed For Freedom* (New York: Boni and Liveright, 1920), p. 57.

190 Zahniser and Fry, *Alice Paul*, 255.

[191] National Woman's Party, *The Suffragist*, 7.

[192] National Woman's Party, *The Suffragist*, cover page.

[193] Rebecca Traister, *Good and Mad: The Revolutionary Power of Women's Anger* (New York: Simon & Schuster Paperbacks, 2018), 239.

[194] Library of Congress, Prints & Photographs Division, photograph by Harris & Ewing, [reproduction number, e.g., LC-USZ62-123456]

[195] Robert H. Ferrell, *Wilson and World War I: 1917-1921* (New York, Harper & Row, 1985), 3.

[196] Rebecca Traister, *Good and Mad*, 239.

[197] Linda G. Ford, *One Woman, One Vote—Rediscovering the Woman Suffrage Movement* (Troutdale, Oregon; NewSage Press, 1995), 127.

[198] National Woman's Party, *The Suffragist*, 6.

[199] National Woman's Party, *The Suffragist*, 5.

[200] Irwin, *The Story*, 488.

[201] Doris Stevens, *Jailed*, 75.

[202] Stanton, et al., *History Vol. II*, 384.

[203] Linda G. Ford, *Alice Paul and the Triumph of Militancy* (Troutdale, OR; NewSage Press; 1995), 176.

[204] National Woman's Party, The Suffragist, cover page.

[205] Ann Bausum, *With Courage and Cloth* (Washington, D.C., National Geographic Society, 2004), 47.

[206] DeWitte Holland, *America in Controversy: History of American Public Address*, (Dubuque: W.C. Brown, 1973), 268.

[207] *Congressional Record-Senate*, Sept. 30, 1918, 10942.

[208] (Congressional Record-Senate, Sept. 30, 1918), 10942.

[209] Holly J. McCammon and Leeann Banaszak, *100 Years of the Nineteenth Amendment: An Appraisal of Women's Political Activism* (New York, NY: Oxford University Press, 2018), 216.

[210] Zahniser and Fry, *Alice Paul*, 319.

[211] Zahniser and Fry, *Alice Paul*, 319.

[212] Weiss, *The Woman's Hour*, 240.

[213] Noel S. Anderson and Haroon Kharem, *Education as Freedom: African American Educational Thought and Activism,* (Lexington Books, Lanham, MD 2009), 47.

[214] Weiss, *The Woman's Hour*, 240.

[215] Weiss, T*he Woman's Hour*, 253.

[216] The New York Times Editorial Staff, *Women's Role* (New York Times Educational Publishing, 2019), 21.

[217] Charlotte Perkins Gilman *The Living of Charlotte Perkins Gilman: An Autobiography* (Madison: University of Wisconsin Press, 1991), 42.

[218] Jennifer Chambers, *Abigail Scott Duniway and Susan B. Anthony in* Oregon (Charleston: The History Press, 2018), 24.

[219] Sally G. McMillen, *Lucy Stone*, 248.

[220] "Frederick Douglass Project Writings: West India Emancipation," University of Rochester, accessed May 5, 2020, https://rbscp.lib.rochester.edu/4398.

[221] *Public Papers of the Presidents of the United States* (Office of the Federal Register National Archives and Records Administration, Washington, D.C.), 1151.

Bibliography

Noel S. Anderson and Haroon Kharem. *Education as Freedom: African American Educational Thought and Activism.* Lanham, MD, Lexington Books; 2009.

Angus, Hilary. "Three Women Who Changed the Course of History on Bicycles." Momentum Magazine. Momentum Magazine Ltd. March 5, 2015. https://momentummag.com/three-women-changed-course-history-bicycle/.

Asante, Molefi Kete and Abu S. Abarry. *African Intellectual Heritage.* Philadelphia, Temple University Press, 1996.

Bausum, Ann. *With Courage and Cloth.* Washington, National Geographic Society, 2004.

Mary Biggs, *Women's Words: The Columbia Book of Quotations by Women.* New York, Chichester, West Sussex; Columbia University Press, 1996.

Blackwell, Alice Stone. *Lucy Stone: Pioneer of Woman Suffragist.* New York, Little, Brown, 1930.

Bloomer, Amelia Jenks and Anne Christine Coon, *Here Me Patiently: The Reform Speeches of Amelia Jenks Bloomer.* Westport, Greenwood Press, 1994.

Brehony, Kathleen A. *After the Darkest Hour: How Suffering Begins the Journey to Wisdom.* New York, Henry Holt, 2000.

Camhi, Jane Jerome. *Women Against Women: American Anti-Suffragism, 1880-1920.* Philadelphia, Carlson Publishing, 1994.

Carroll, Andrew. *Letters of a Nation: A Collection of Extraordinary American Letters.* New York, Broadway Books, 1997.

Catt, Carrie Chapman. "The Crisis" speech. New York, National American Woman Suffrage Association Convention, 1916.

Chambers, Jennifer. *Abilgail Scott Duniway and Susan B. Anthony in Oregon: Hesitate No Longer.* Charleston, The History Press, 2018.

Chandler, Robin M. *Women, War, and Violence: Personal Perspectives and Global Activism.* New York, Palgrave MacMillian, 2010.

Cherif, Feryal M. *Myths About Women's Rights: How, Where, and Why Rights Advance.* New York, Oxford University Press, 2015.

Clinton, William J. *Public Papers of the Presidents of the United States: William J. Clinton,*

200-2001 (In Three Books) Book I—January 1 to June 26, 2000. District of Columbia, US Government Printing Office, Office of the Federal Register National Archives and Records Administration, 2001.

Cobrin, Pamela. *From Winning the Vote to Directing on Broadway: The Emergence of Women on the New York Stage, 1880-1927.* Newark, University of Delaware Press, 2009.

Collins, Joseph. "Lucretia Mott—Force for Equality." Last modified January 6, 2017. http://infinitefire.org/info/lucretia-mott-force-for-equality/.

Colman, Penny. *Elizabeth Cady Stanton and Susan B. Anthony: A Friendship that Changed the World.* New York, Henry Holt, 2011.

"Compare the Two Speeches." The Sojourner Truth Project. Accessed May 1, 2020. https://www.thesojournertruthproject.com/compare-the-speeches.

Congressional Record, 65th Cong., 1st Sess. 1918. Washington, DC.

Cooney, Robert P.J. Jr. *Winning the Vote: The Triumph of the American Woman Suffrage Movement.* Half Moon Bay, CA, American Graphic Press, 2005.

Douglass-Chin, Richard J. *Preacher Woman Sings the Blues: The Autobiographies of Nineteenth-Century African American Evangelists.* Columbia, University of Missouri Press, 2001.

DuBois, W.E.B. "Woman Suffrage," *The Crisis* vol. 9, no. 6 (1915) 285. The Modernists Journals Project. Brown and Tulsa Universities, ongoing.

Faulkner, Carol. *Lucretia Mott's Heresy.* Philadelphia, University of Pennsylvania Press, 2011.

Ferrell, Robert H. *Wilson and World War I: 1917-1921.* New York, Harper & Row, 1985.

Ford, Linda G. *Alice Paul and the Triumph of Militancy.* Troutdale, NewSage Press, 1995.

Ford, Linda G. *Iron-Jawed Angels: The Suffrage Militancy of the National Woman's Party, 1912-1920.* Lanham, University Press of America, 1991.

Ford, Linda G. *One Woman, One Vote—Rediscovering the Woman Suffrage Movement.* Troutdale, NewSage Press, 1995.

Fredericks, Carrie. *Amendment XIX: Granting Women the Right to Vote.* New Haven, Greenhaven Press, 2009.

Frost-Knappman, Elizabeth and Kathryn Cullen-Dupont, *Women's Suffrage in America: An Eyewitness History.* New York, Facts On File, 1992.

Fry, Amelia, "Audio Interview," Alice Paul Institute, May 12, 1973, http://www.alicepaul.org/audio-interview/. Via Erin, Sawadzki at Alice Paul Institute.

Gabriel, Mary. *Notorious Victoria: The Uncensored Life of Victoria Woodhull.* Chapel Hill, Algonquin Books, 1998.

Gage, Frances. New York Independent (New York), April 23, 1863. Accessed August 8, 2019. https://voicesofdemocracy.umd.edu/truth-address-at-the-womans-rights-convention-textual-authentication/.

Gage, Matilda Joslyn. *Woman, Church & State: The Original Exposé of Male Against the Female Sex.* Charles H. Kerr, Chicago, 1893.

Gage, Matilda Joslyn. "Women Rebels." *The National Citizen and Ballot Box Volume 5, No. 1.* Syracuse, May 1880.

Gilman, Charlotte Perkins. *The Living of Charlotte Perkins Gilman: An* Autobiography. Madison, University of Wisconsin Press, 1991.

Goodman, Ellen and Patricia O'Brien. *I Know Just What You Mean: The Power of Friendship in Women's Lives.* New York, Fireside, 2000.

Gordon, Ann D. *The Selected Papers of Elizabeth Cady Stanton and Susan B. Anthony Volume III.* New Brunswick, Rutgers University Press, 2003.

Grana, Sheryl J. Women and Justice. Lanham, MD; Rowman & Littlefield; 2010.

Grand, Sarah. *Ideala: A Study From Life,* ed. Molly Youngkin. Kansas City, Valancourt Books, 2008.

Green, Elna C. *Southern Strategies: Southern Women and the Woman Suffrage Question.* Chapel Hill, The University of North Carolina Press, 1997.

Griffith, Elisabeth. *In Her Own Right,* New York, Oxford University Press, 1984.

Harper, Ida Husted. *The Life and Work of Susan B. Anthony Volumes I & II.* Indianapolis and Kansas City, Bowen-Merrill, 1898.

Harris & Ewing, Washington, D.C. Lincoln's birthday. On the banners during Congressional debate on whether we should enter the war. United States, 1917. Photograph. https://www.loc.gov/item/mnwp000226/.

Helton, Edwina and Jeffrey Jones, The American Suffragette's Journey to Enfranchisement: From Seneca Falls to Ratification of the Nineteenth Amendment. Minnetonka,

MN; Meadowbrook Publishing; 2018.

Higginson, T. W. "Marriage of Lucy Stone Under Protest." The Liberator, vol. 25, no. 18 (Whole no. 1085) History is a Weapon. Accessed August 3, 2019. https://www.historyisaweapon.com/defcon1/stoneblackwellmarriageprotest.html

Hoff, Joan. Rights of Passage: The Past and Future of the ERA. Bloomington, Indiana University Press, 1986.

Holland, DeWitte. *America in Controversy: History of American Public Address.* Dubuque, W.C. Brown, 1973.

Irwin, Inez Haynes. *The Story of Alice Paul and the National Woman's Party.* Fairfax, Denlinger's Publishers, 1977.

Kelly, Colleen E. and Anna L. Eblen, *Women Who Speak for Peace.* Lanham, Rowman & Littlefield, 2002.

Kendall, Martha E. *Failure is Impossible!: The History of American Women's Rights.* Minneapolis, Lerner Publications, 2001.

Kerr, Andrea Moore. *Lucy Stone: Speaking Out for Equality.* New Brunswick, Rutgers University Press, 1992.

Kroeger, Brooke. *The Suffragents: How Women Used Men to Get the Vote.* Albany, State University of New York, 2017.

Lewis, David Levering. *W. E. B. Du Bois: Biography of a Race 1868–1919.* New York, Henry Holt, 1993.

Library of Congress, Prints & Photographs Division, photograph by Harris & Ewing, [reproduction number, e.g., LC-USZ62-123456].

Love, Bettina. *We Want to Do More Than Survive: Abolitionist Teaching and the Pursuit of Educational Freedom.* Boston, Beacon Press, 2019.

Lumsden, Linda J. *Inez: The Life and Times of Inez Milholland.* Bloomington & Indianapolis, Indiana University Press, 2016.

Mabee, Carleton with Susan Mabee Newhouse. *Sojourner Truth: Slave, Prophet, Legend.* New York and London, NYU Press, 1995.

Macy, Sue. *Wheels of Change: How Women Rode the Bicycle to Freedom (With a Few Flat Tires Along The Way).* Washington, D.C., National Geographic Children's Books, Reprint

Edition, February 7, 2017.

Maryanski, Maureen. *The "Suff Bird Women" and Woodrow Wilson* (March 26, 2014, blog. NYHistory.org/the-suff-bird-women-and-woodrow-wilson.

McCammon, Holly J. and Banaszak, Leann. *100 Years of the Nineteenth Amendment: An Appraisal of Women's Political Activism.* New York, NY, Oxford University Press, 2018.

McMillen, Sally G. *Lucy Stone: An Unapologetic Life.* New York, Oxford University Press, 2015.

Miller, D. Douglas. *Drumore Quakers' Precious Habitation.* Bloomington, Xlibris Publishing, 2016.

Minor v. Happersett, 88 U.S. (21 Wall.) 162 (1875).

Mott, Lucretia, Lucy Stone, and National American Woman Suffrage Association Collection. *Discourse on Woman.* Philadelphia: T.B. Peterson, 1850. Pdf. https://www.loc.gov/item/09002748/.

Nardo, Don. *The Split History of the Women's Suffrage Movement: Suffragists' Perspective.* North Mankato, MN, Compass Point Books, 2014.

National Association Opposed To Woman Suffrage. *Some reasons why we oppose votes for women ... National association opposed to woman suffrage. New York City.* New York, 1894. Pdf. https://www.loc.gov/item/rbpe.13001300c/.

National Woman's Party, Textile Collection, Catalog #1913.033," 1913–1920. https://nationalwomansparty.pastperfectonline.com/webobject/1925C56F-9310-4E84-A67D-179389594096.

National Woman's Party, *The Suffragist.* Washington D.C., June 23, 1917. Accessed January 7, 2020. https://www.alicepaul.org/.

Neejer, Christine. "Cycling and women's rights in the suffrage press." (2011). *Electronic Theses and Dissertations.* Paper 1047. https://doi.org/10.18297/etd/1047.

Nelson, Carolyn Christensen. *The New Woman Reader: Fiction, Articles, Drama of the 1890s* (Ontario: Broadview Press, 2001), 141.

Owen, Karen L. *The Women Officeholders and the Role Models Who Pioneered the Way.* Lanham, Lexington Books, 2017.

Payne, Karen. *Between Ourselves: Letters Between Mothers and Daughters 1750-1982.* Boston, Houghton Mifflin, 1984.

Petranovic, Danilo, Ralph Lerner, and Benjamin A. Kleinerman. *The Writings of Abraham Lincoln*. New Haven, Yale University Press, 2012.

Podell, Leslie. "Compare the Two Speeches," The Sojourner Truth Project. Accessed August 8, 2019. https://www.thesojournertruthproject.com/compare-the-speeches.

Popova, Maria. "A List of Don'ts for Women on Bicycles Circa 1895," Brain Pickings. January 3, 2012. https://www.brainpickings.org/2012/01/03/donts-for-women-on-bicycles-1895/.

Rappaport, Helen. *Encyclopedia of Women Social Reformers*. Santa Barbara, ABC-CLIO, 2001.

Russell, Anna. *So Here I Am: Speeches by Great Women to Empower and Inspire*. London, White Lion Publishing, 2019.

Schwartz, Heather E. *Girls Rebel!: Amazing Tales of Women Who Broke the Mold*. North Mankato, MN, Capstone Press, 2015.

Scutts, Joanna. "Women Cycling Groups Feminism History We Bike." Curbed, VOX Media, May 15, 2019. https://www.curbed.com/2019/5/15/18618037/women-cycling-groups-feminism-history-we-bike.

Sherr, Lynn. *Failure Is Impossible: Susan B. Anthony In Her Own Words*. New York, Times Books, 1995.

Signorielli, Nancy. *Women in Communication: A Biographical Sourcebook*. Westport, Greenwood Press, 1996.

Sprading, Charles T. *Liberty and the Great Libertarians*. Los Angeles, Golden Press, 2015.

Stanton, Elizabeth Cady. *Declaration of Rights and Sentiments*. Rochester, NY Printed by John Dick at the North Star Office 1848. New York Heritage Digital Collections. https://cdm16694.contentdm.oclc.org/digital/collection/p16694coll96/id/52.

Stanton, Elizabeth Cady. *Eighty Years and More: Reminiscences 1857-1897*. New York, Shocken Books, 1971.

Stanton, Elizabeth Cady. *The Woman's Bible Volume I*. New York, European Publishing, 1895.

Stanton, Elizabeth Cady, Susan B. Anthony, Matilda Joslyn Gage, and Ida Hustad Harper. *History of Woman Suffrage Volumes I-VI*. Rochester, Charles Mann, 1887 & 1895.

Stanton, Theodore and Harriot Stanton Blatch, eds. *Elizabeth Cady Stanton as Revealed in Her Letters, Diary, and Reminiscences*. 2 volumes. New York, Harper & Brothers, 1922.

Stevens, Doris. *Jailed For Freedom.* New York, Boni and Liveright, 1920.

Suffrage envoy Sara Bard Field left and her driver, Maria Kindberg center, and machinist Ingeborg Kindstedt right during their cross-country journey to present suffrage petitions to Congress, September-December. United States Washington D.C, 1915. [Sept.-Dec] Photograph. https://www.loc.gov/item/mnwp000424/.

Szczepanski, Carolyn. "Women's Bike History: Kittie Knox," The League of American Bicyclists. League of American Wheelmen, Inc. *dba* League of American Bicyclists, March 8, 2013. https://www.bikeleague.org/content/womens-bike-history-kittie-knox.

Terrell, Mary Church, Columbia Theatre, Daniel Murray Pamphlet Collection, and African American Pamphlet Collection. *The Progress of Colored Women.* [Washington, D.C., Smith Brothers, Printers, 1898] Pdf. https://www.loc.gov/item/90898298/.

The New York Times Editorial Staff, *Women's Role.* New York, New York Times Educational Publishing, 2019.

Todd, Anne M. *Susan B. Anthony: Activist (Women of Achievement).* Philadelphia, Chelsea House Publications, 2009.

Traister, Rebecca. *Good and Mad: The Revolutionary Power of Women's Anger.* New York, Simon & Schuster Paperbacks, 2018.

Underwood, Benjamin Franklin. *The Free Religious Index Vol. I, New Series No. 5, Thursday, July 29, 1880.* Boston, MA, 245.

Van Voris, Jacqueline. *Carrie Chapman Catt: A Public Life.* New York, The Feminist Press, City University of New York, 1987.

Venet, Wendy Hamand. *Neither Ballots or Bullets: Women Abolitionists and The Civil War.* Charlottesville, University of Virginia Press, 1991.

Waldman, Michael. *The Fight to Vote.* New York, Simon & Schuster, 2016.

Watkins, Valethia. "Votes for Women: Race, Gender, and W.E.B. DuBois's Advocacy of Woman Suffrage," *Phylon: The Clark Atlanta University Review of Race and Culture*, Vol. 53, No. 2, 2016.

Weber, Sandra. *The Woman Suffrage Statue: A History of Adelaide Johnson's Portrait Monument to Lucretia Mott, Elizabeth Cady Stanton and Susan B. Anthony at the United States Capitol.* Jefferson, NC; McFarland; 2016.

Weber, Sandra. "How Long Must Women Wait," The New York History Blog, last modified

October 27, 2016. https://newyorkalmanack.com/2016/10/sandra-weber-how-long-must-women-wait/.

Weekes, Karen. *Women Know Everything!: 3,241 Quips, Quotes, & Brilliant Remarks.* Philadelphia, Quirk Books, 2007.

Weiss, Elaine. *The Woman's Hour: The Great Fight to Win the Vote.* New York, Viking, 2018.

Wellman, Judith. *The Road to Seneca Falls: Elizabeth Cady Stanton and the First Woman's Rights Convention.* Champaign, University of Illinois Press, 2004.

Wilson, Woodrow. *Wilson, Volume IV: Confusions and Crises, 1915-1916.* Princeton, Princeton University Press, 1964.

Woman's Rights Convention, Lucy Stone, National American Woman Suffrage Association Collection, and Susan B. Anthony Collection. *The proceedings of the Woman's Rights Convention, held at Worcester, October 15th and 16th.* New York, Published for the Committee by Fowlers and Wells, 1852. Pdf. https://www.loc.gov/item/93838287/.

Zahniser, J.D. and Amelia R. Fry. Alice Paul: Claiming Power. New York, Oxford University Press, 2014.